Forgery

Gail B. Stewart
AR B.L.: 9.4
Points: 4.0   UG

Forgery

Other titles in Lucent's Crime Scene Investigations series include:

Arson

The Birmingham Church Bombing

Bombings

The DC Sniper Shootings

The Forensic Anthropologist

Forgery

The Medical Examiner

Murder in Mississippi: The 1964 Freedom Summer Killings

Murder

T 32393

L

Forgery

by Gail B. Stewart

LUCENT BOOKS

An imprint of Thomson Gale, a part of The Thomson Corporation

THOMSON
*
GALE ™

Detroit • New York • San Francisco • New Haven, Conn. • Waterville, Maine • London

LIBRARY OF CONGRESS CATALOGING-IN-PUBLICATION DATA

Stewart, Gail, 1949–
Forgery / by Gail B. Stewart.
    p. cm. — (Crime scene investigations series)
Includes bibliographical references and index.
ISBN-13: 978-1-59018-949-8 (hardcover : alk. paper)
ISBN-10: 1-59018-949-3 (hardcover : alk. paper)
1. Forgery—Juvenile literature. 2.   Fraud—Juvenile literature.   I. Title. II. Series.

HV6675.S84 2007
363.25'963—dc22
                                                          2006017277

Printed in the United States of America

Contents

Foreword

The popularity of crime scene and investigative crime shows on television has come as a surprise to many who work in the field. The main surprise is the concept that crime scene analysts are the true crime solvers, when in truth, it takes dozens of people, doing many different jobs, to solve a crime. Often, the crime scene analyst's contribution is a small one. One Minnesota forensic scientist says that the public "has gotten the wrong idea. Because I work in a lab similar to the ones on *CSI*, people seem to think I'm solving crimes left and right—just me and my microscope. They don't believe me when I tell them that it's the investigators that are solving crimes, not me."

Crime scene analysts do have an important role to play, however. Science has rapidly added a whole new dimension to gathering and assessing evidence. Modern crime labs can match a hair of a murder suspect to one found on a murder victim, for example, or recover a latent fingerprint from a threatening letter, or use a powerful microscope to match tool marks made during the wiring of an explosive device to a tool in a suspect's possession.

Probably the most exciting of the forensic scientist's tools is DNA analysis. DNA can be found in just one drop of blood, a dribble of saliva on a toothbrush, or even the residue from a fingerprint. Some DNA analysis techniques enable scientists to tell with certainty, for example, whether a drop of blood on a suspect's shirt is that of a murder victim.

While these exciting techniques are now an essential part of many investigations, they cannot solve crimes alone. "DNA doesn't come with a name and address on it," says the Minnesota forensic scientist. "It's great if you have someone in custody to match the sample to, but otherwise, it doesn't help. That's the investigator's job. We can have all the great DNA evidence in the world, and without a suspect, it will just sit on the shelf. We've all seen cases with very little forensic evidence get solved by the resourcefulness of a detective."

While forensic specialists get the most media attention today, the work of detectives still forms the core of most criminal investigations. Their job, in many ways, has changed little over the years. Most cases are still solved through the persistence and determination of a criminal detective whose work may be anything but glamorous. Many cases require routine, even mind-numbing tasks. After the July 2005 bombings in London, for example, police officers sat in front of video players watching thousands of hours of closed-circuit television tape from security cameras throughout the city, and as a result were able to get the first images of the bombers.

The Lucent Books Crime Scene Investigations series explores the variety of ways crimes are solved. Titles cover particular crimes such as murder, specific cases such as the killing of three civil rights workers in Mississippi, or the role specialists such as medical examiners play in solving crimes. Each title in the series demonstrates the ways a crime may be solved, from the various applications of forensic science and technology to the reasoning of investigators. Sidebars examine both the limits and possibilities of the new technologies and present crime statistics, career information, and step-by-step explanations of scientific and legal processes.

The Crime Scene Investigations series strives to be both informative and realistic about how members of law enforcement—criminal investigators, forensic scientists, and others—solve crimes, for it is essential that student researchers understand that crime solving is rarely quick or easy. Many factors—from a detective's dogged pursuit of one tenuous lead to a suspect's careless mistakes to sheer luck to complex calculations computed in the lab—are all part of crime solving today.

An Almost Invisible Crime

When an elderly Minneapolis woman received her bank statement in late 2005, she was startled. "My account was down $1,000," recalls Patricia. "I called the bank manager. I thought they had made a mistake, because I've never spent that much money in a month."

She says that the manager verified that the statement was accurate. "I'm a widow," she says. "No one else but me writes checks on that account." But when the manager looked more closely, he found that five checks for two hundred dollars each had been written on the account. "That was it," Patricia says. "The name was someone I'd never heard of, and the signatures were not even close to mine. Somebody had stolen five blank checks from my purse and wrote the checks out to himself and signed my name—and then he cashed them."[1]

All Kinds of Forgery

Patricia was the victim of a forger—someone who creates a copy of something real (in this case, a personal check) for the purpose of defrauding another. And while check forgery is a growing concern in the United States, it is by no means the only type of forgery. There are forgers of historical documents, religious artifacts, and classic works of art. People have also forged lottery tickets and handicap parking permits.

There are even forgers of sports memorabilia, as one Milwaukee man found out in February 2006. Kevin Demitros participated in an online auction for a rare baseball card bearing the printed signatures of four of the first five players inducted into baseball's Hall of Fame—Babe Ruth, Walter Johnson, Honus Wagner, and Ty Cobb. He won the auction, and paid eighty-five thousand dollars for the card, saying that he looked at the purchase as a retirement investment.

His excitement dwindled, however, when he saw a television program about forgery in sports and celebrity memorabilia. He had his new card studied by document analysts, who suspected that at least two of the signatures were fake. After getting the experts' report, Demitros said, "I was sick to my stomach."[2]

Not Just for Money

For most forgers, money is the motive. Certainly, the crook who forges another's name on a check, or who sells a baseball card whose signatures have been faked, is trying to get rich at someone else's expense. However, there are other motives for forgery, too.

Baseball enthusiast Kevin Demitros spent thousands of dollars on this signed card, only to learn that it might be a forgery.

Some art forgers say that they created copies only to see if they could do it and get away with it. They insist that they find it exhilarating to create a painting under the name of a famous artist that fools even the experts. A literary forger, William Henry Ireland, had the same motivation when he claimed to have discovered a Shakespearean play called *Vortigern and Rowena*. The news of the discovery was exciting, but the play Ireland had forged was not good enough to fool anyone familiar with Shakespeare's work.

Other forgers are motivated by the need to change or control history, such as the creator of the phony Hitler diaries in 1983. Experts believe that while the forger and his accomplice were motivated partly by the millions of dollars magazines and newspapers would pay to publish the diaries, the two were also sympathetic to Hitler. The diaries therefore presented an Adolf Hitler that was both compassionate and kindly—a true change of history.

Perhaps one of the most worrisome motives for forgery is terrorism. After the attacks on the World Trade Center and Pentagon on September 11, 2001, investigators began learning how easy it had been for a number of al-Qaeda terrorists to use forging skills to create phony passports so that they could enter the United States without arousing suspicion. Said terrorist expert Judge Jean Louis Bruguire, "For these groups, passports are as important as weapons."[3]

"Forgers Do Their Thing in Private"

For those investigating forgery, the task is difficult on a number of levels. First, the crime is virtually invisible when it is committed. "Forgers do their thing in private," says one police officer. "It's not violent and it's not loud—it's just a guy quietly forging a check or whatever. And when he cashes the check, let's say, it's not often identified as a forgery right on the spot. Someone eventually notices, but by that time—maybe it's hours or days later—the guy is long gone."[4]

CEDULA DE IDENTIDAD PERSONAL No. 5-1- 0054830

Nombre y apellido _Luis Alonso Martínez Flores_

Fecha de Nacimiento _20 Junio 1973_   Lugar de Nacimiento _San Dionisio Usulután_

Salvadoreño por _Nacimiento_

Nombre y apellido del Padre _Oscar Fermelio Martínez Cruz_ apellido de la Madre _Marina del C. Montano_

Estado Civil _Soltero_   Nombre y apellido del Cónyuge _____

Residencia _Col. Puerta El Sol 2 pje. Casa No 4_

Profesión u Oficio _Jornalero_   Servicio Militar _____

Sabe Leer y Escribir _Si_   Grado Militar _____

Sabe Firmar _Si_

Estatura _1.61 (in Cmts.)_

Peso _56 (En Kgs.)_

Color de la Piel _Morena_

Color de los Ojos _Café_

Color del Pelo _Negro_

Señales Especiales _Ninguna_

Firma: _Luis Martínez_

Municipio de **USULUTAN**   Departamento de **USULUTAN**

Fecha _8 de Julio • 1991_

The other difficulty is just as problematic. Because of the priority of solving rapes, murders, and other violent crimes, police departments in many cities around the United States have less and less money for forgery and fraud units. "We're swamped with more cases than ever, and we've got almost one-third fewer people on the job," says one detective, "but we do catch quite a few of these people."[5]

Tracking down a forger first requires identifying whether the item in question is in fact a forgery—often a very intricate process. Part of this process involves forensic lab work, such as testing the chemical makeup of paper and ink on a historical manuscript or trying to date the canvas of a painting to see if it could be as old as it is purported to be. The lab can also

Pictured is the identity card of a man who forged passports used by the September 11 terrorists to enter the United States.

11

help once a forgery has been identified—from scrutinizing security tape from a bank to get a clearer image of a forger to coaxing a latent fingerprint from a forged check.

"One Time Too Many"

As valuable as the forensic lab is, however, it is the investigators who provide the leadership in solving the case. Depending on the type of forgery, a case often requires the expertise of a historian, a banker, or an art expert. It is then up to the investigator to coordinate the expert opinion with what has been learned in the crime lab. It is also very helpful to get information from possible witnesses and to study any new cases of forgery that bear a close resemblance to the current one.

All of that, and sometimes a bit of luck, says one officer, can lead to an arrest. "You know, sometimes the bad guys just try it one time too many," says another. "It's a good day for everybody when we put them out of business."[6]

CHAPTER 1

Forging and Bank Fraud

Gary did not realize he was a victim until the day after the crime was committed. "I parked at a downtown garage," he says.

> I stupidly left my checkbook on the seat of my car—I didn't even think about it. But while I was gone, someone broke into my car and stole the checkbook.
>
> They didn't break a window—just used one of those illegal wires—the ones you can just slide through a crack in the window, you know? The car door was kind of ajar when I got back, but I thought maybe I had just been careless and didn't notice that it hadn't closed tight. Anyway, I didn't figure it out until the next day, when I was looking for my checkbook. I thought maybe it had slid down into a crevice or under the seat of the car or something. But no, it wasn't there.[7]

Televisions and iPods

Realizing then that the checkbook was either stolen or lost, Gary called his bank. "They froze the account," he recalls, "so they'd know that any checks written on my account from then on weren't being written by me." The following day, his banker informed Gary that checks for more than forty-five hundred dollars had been written on his account over the past two days. "Most were out of state," he says. "They bought televisions and iPods and stuff like that. Evidently no one thought to ask for an ID—or maybe the cashiers didn't even really look at the ID the guy had. I was really angry, but glad I wasn't going to get charged for those checks. It taught me a huge lesson. I'll never be careless with my checkbook again."[8]

"It's Called Identity Theft"

The person who forged Gary's name in order to pay for thousands of dollars of electronic equipment was engaging in one of the most devious of financial crimes. "It's one type of forgery called identity theft," explains bank fraud investigator Vicki Colliander. "Identity theft occurs every time someone signs your name, uses your personal information such as a social security number or checking account information—and check fraud is the type of identity theft bankers see most often."[9]

Thieves have a much harder time getting information off shredded documents.

The cost of check fraud is enormous—1.4 million fraudulent checks are passed each business day, resulting in $10 billion of loss to banks, retailers, and consumers each year. The problem is getting worse, too. Financial experts say that since 2002 check fraud has increased at a rate of 2.5 percent per year. Notes one frustrated investigator, "It's a huge, huge issue, and the problem is growing like crazy."[10]

By the Numbers

$815 MILLION

Amount of check washing done each year by forgers.

"Hopefully We Can Get the Cavalry There in Time"

Investigators say that cases of check forgery are sometimes solved by an alert retail clerk. "Most retail stores ask for ID for a personal check," says Minneapolis police lieutenant Steve Kincaid.

But a lot of workers in the checkout lane aren't really paying attention. They just kind of glance at it and that's it. And that's why so many forged checks can get by unnoticed. But we also have cases of cashiers who are more careful, and realize that that driver's license does not have the same information as the check. Sometimes they even sign the name wrong—misspell it or something. These guys aren't that smart.

When that happens, the cashier at Wal-Mart or Target or whatever store, alerts store security and they call us. The store security will try to hold them until a squad can respond. Hopefully we can get the cavalry there in time to grab them. Sometimes a clerk will stall them by saying that the computers are down and the customer should come back in half an hour to pick up

the items he purchased. You'd be surprised—some of these guys are dumb enough to come back.[11]

Knowing the Forger

Often investigators can determine who the forger might be by understanding the circumstances of the victim. In a surprisingly large number of cases, a forger often turns out to be known to the victim. In fact, in about 20 percent of such cases, a family member is responsible for the forgery. "It may be an older child with a drug or gambling problem, or something like that," says Colliander. "In cases like these, a victim often suspects that might be the case, and may be unwilling to have us pursue the investigation. In that situation, the victim will take the loss."

Occasionally, however, parents who suspect their own child of forging a check say that they prefer to continue the investigation. "It's like a 'tough love' thing," Colliander continues.

"They'll tell us, 'You know, we've gone through this before and we've been unsuccessful with dealing with our son or whatever—so go ahead.' It all depends."[12]

In other cases, knowing that the victim was disabled or elderly might provide a clue. "It isn't surprising that the vulnerable in our society are targets of crimes like this," says Joleen, an advocate for the elderly. "They might depend on a home health worker to come in, or a neighbor to get groceries or pick up medication from the drug store. And instead of doing their work honestly, they take advantage. Often when the neighbor or home health worker is confronted, they admit to what they've done."[13]

Bank officials say that while stolen and forged checks are common, they rarely become a high-profile crime, simply because the dollar amounts involved are seldom high. "Once someone realizes their checkbook is gone, or that a few checks have been stolen, we freeze the account," says investigator Colliander. "These forged signatures or stolen checks are definitely a nuisance, but the dollar value tends to be low."[14]

New Types of Forgery

What has bankers and police more worried are variations of forgery that are more advanced types of identity theft. One of these variations is carried out by crooks who chemically alter checks that have already been filled out and then rewrite those checks to themselves. Known as "check washing," this crime has become more and more common in recent years.

To obtain checks, crooks steal outgoing mail. Police call the theft "red-flagging," because the crooks look for home mailboxes on which the little red flag has been raised to alert the postal carrier that there is mail to be picked up. Victims are usually unaware of the crime until a creditor sends a notice that the previous month's bill was not paid—and by that time, the thief has moved to another neighborhood, stealing checks from someone else's mailbox.

One Seattle woman, a self-employed artist, had nearly twelve thousand dollars emptied from her bank account when thieves intercepted outgoing bills with checks inside from her home mailbox. "It was my business and personal account," she says. "It was all the money I had."[15]

Jesse, a postal carrier, says that he never used to think twice about putting the red flag up on his own mailbox. "Signaling for a mail pickup is real convenient," he says. "You don't have to double park your car to mail a letter on the street. But you hear about it so often now, it's pretty frightening. Someone said that it's like telling a thief, 'Hey, I got outgoing bills here—checks are right inside!' With that kind of stuff going on, I'd never let outgoing mail sit all day in my mailbox. Nobody should—it's just tempting fate."[16]

If the process of finding ready-made checks is easy, the process of washing them is not much more difficult. A number of easily obtained chemicals can be used to erase most inks from stolen checks. After applying the chemical to the key parts of the check, the crook can make it out to a name for which he or she has a fake ID, for any amount of money.

"It's Discouraging for Everyone"

"The ID thing is real common," says one investigator.

They're available online for pretty cheap. . . . The companies that sell them have a disclaimer, saying that they're novelty items. But it's no surprise that these IDs—fake drivers licenses, mostly—can fool a lot of people.

Plus, there are lots of bad guys who are pretty good at making their own, with a laminating machine and computer. The legit IDs have a number of features that are

This mail carrier assisted the FBI in locating a check forger during a 1941 investigation. Check fraud continues to be a common crime.

The Problem of Identity Theft and Fraud

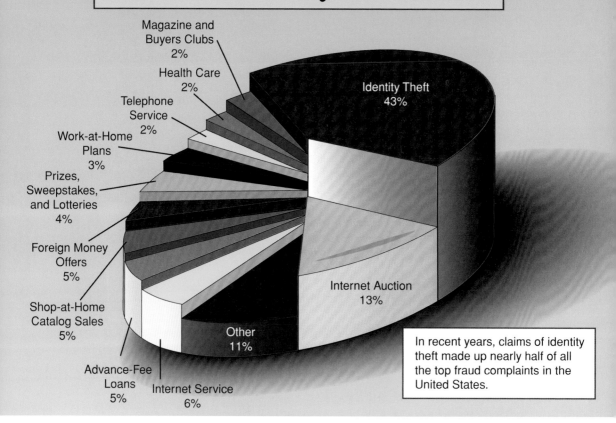

Magazine and Buyers Clubs 2%

Health Care 2%

Telephone Service 2%

Work-at-Home Plans 3%

Prizes, Sweepstakes, and Lotteries 4%

Foreign Money Offers 5%

Shop-at-Home Catalog Sales 5%

Advance-Fee Loans 5%

Internet Service 6%

Other 11%

Internet Auction 13%

Identity Theft 43%

In recent years, claims of identity theft made up nearly half of all the top fraud complaints in the United States.

supposed to separate the real from the fake. . . . But it seems like no sooner does the DMV [Department of Motor Vehicles] come up with a new foolproof design, there are fakes out there with the holograms and all the rest. It's discouraging for everyone in law enforcement.[17]

One woman was so skilled at the technique of washing checks that she roamed through city streets with a check-washing lab in her car. Not only did she have the necessary chemicals for obliterating the name of the person to whom the check was originally made out, she also had a laptop computer, printer, and laminating machine. Each time she was successful at stealing outgoing bills from a home mailbox and washing the checks inside, she forged a new identification on a driver's license—each with her own photograph, but with a new fake name and address.

Making Homemade Checks

Another variation on check forgery can be accomplished with a computer scanner and printer. This technology can enable forgers to create their own checks—ones that look completely legitimate to most people.

Forgers can create almost any sort of check—personal checks or business checks—using software programs for check printing that are perfectly legal. "Office supply stores all over the country sell that stuff, because many small businesses print their own checks," explains Colliander. "You can buy check paper stock that looks exactly like the paper bank checks are printed on, too. The technology is out there—it's just that crooks have found a way to use it for illegal purposes."[18]

Like those who wash checks, the crooks who make these homemade checks rely on real account numbers, which they get from red-flagged home mailboxes as well as a host of other sources. "We had a group of check counterfeiters not long ago who were getting account numbers from some guys working in a local sandwich shop," says one police officer.

> People would go in there and pay for their lunch with a check, and the guy and his son who ran the place were Xeroxing the checks and selling the account numbers to a check ring. The ones making the checks didn't need the actual checks or the name of the person. All that was going to be changed anyhow once they started making the check. But they had a legitimate account number. And they'd been doing this for months, and no one had any idea that their personal account information had been compromised."[19]

"A Big, Humongous Problem"

By creating real-looking checks and cashing them under a variety of names, such check forgers are often difficult to catch. They do not call attention to themselves by making the same mistakes other forgers do. They have identification, they do not use the same account or name for more than a check or two, and they do not usually give in to the temptation of making a check amount suspiciously high.

But while the check amounts are not generally high, the quantity of fraudulent checks is staggering. In 2000 one check forgery ring in Minneapolis had already cashed more than $1.5 million in bad checks, and police still had not caught them. One officer believed that before the ring was arrested, they would probably double that amount. "On any given afternoon they print out a couple dozen checks and cash in $15,000 to $20,000," said Lieutenant Dana Smyser in April 2000. "Unfortunately, they're still operating and making more money as we speak. It's a big, humongous problem."[20]

What the Experts Look For

However, many check forgery rings do eventually get caught, and police say that their arrests come about for a number of reasons. One of the most common is someone spotting a fraudulent check at the point at which it is being cashed. According to the American Bankers Association, it is often the sharp eye of an alert bank teller who spots the forgery before the crook gets the cash and flees.

Several aspects of a check are important for a teller to note. One is the sequence of numbers on the bottom of every check. Far from being a random combination, the numbers indicate not only the checking account number, but the Federal Reserve number of the issuing bank. The United States is divided into twelve different Federal Reserve Districts, and each district is identified by a number.

The first number on the numeric sequence tells the district number—which should match up with the location of the bank. If the first number is an 11, for example, that means that the bank account originates in the eleventh Federal Reserve district, which includes Texas and parts of Louisiana and New Mexico. However, if the check shows the bank as one in

Meth and Identity Theft

Most identity theft investigators feel that the primary motivator behind that crime can be summed up with one word: meth. The drug is rampant, especially in rural areas, and is highly addictive. Being part of counterfeit check rings is one of the easiest ways for users to make the money they need for their drug habit.

Many work as mail thieves, stealing outgoing mail from home mailboxes. Others troll behind office buildings and search through dumpsters, looking for bank statements with account numbers, social security numbers, or other sensitive information. Even those who dutifully shred their credit card information may not be safe, say police. It is common for those high on meth, a drug that often produces a burst of energy that can last between eighteen and twenty-four hours, to tackle mind-numbing tasks, such as piecing together shredded documents in order to steal identity information.

An Indiana State Police trooper displays paraphernalia confiscated during a methamphetamine lab bust.

Chicago, the counterfeiter evidently did not do his or her homework. "A teller would know that detail," says Colliander, "and if that number didn't match up with the bank on the check, that's a sign that something's wrong."[21]

Sometimes the printing on the check does not seem to be aligned very well, says one bank teller, or the color of the checks seems wrong. "I had a customer who brought in a payroll check from a large store—one of several in town here," she explains. "And I see those checks all the time—they're always kind of a light green. And this one was green, but it wasn't the same. That was the only thing that looked wrong. It ended up that it was counterfeit."[22]

In hopes of avoiding thefts, restaurants like this one often post bad checks where employees will see them.

Fuzzy Checks and Misspelled Words

Another teller says that he has spotted several fraudulent checks that had misspelled words printed on them. "On one, they misspelled the name of the bank—which seemed amazingly

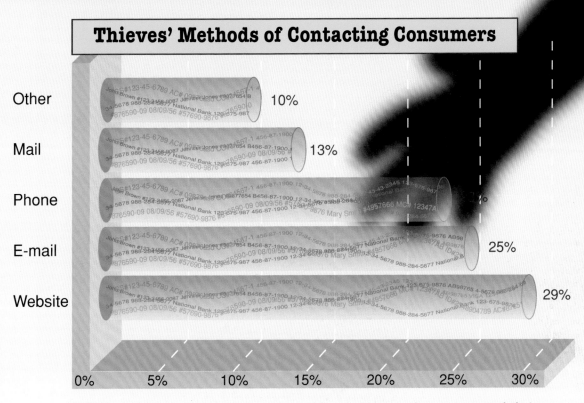

Thieves' Methods of Contacting Consumers

Other	10%
Mail	13%
Phone	
E-mail	25%
Website	29%

0% 5% 10% 15% 20% 25% 30%

In cases of identity theft and other types of fraud, thieves gain access to a victim's funds through various methods. Most often the victims of scams are contacted by phone, email, or the internet.

dumb," he says. "On another one they spelled a street name wrong. I think without the misspellings, those checks might have just gone through, because other than that, the checks looked fine."[23]

While most of the clues to counterfeit checks are visual, the feel of a check can sometimes be an indication that the check is fraudulent—especially a washed check. Washed checks may not look suspicious, but the chemicals used by the forger affect the texture of the paper. Says investigator Colliander, "They have kind of a fuzzy feel. You run your hand over a legitimate check, and it's very smooth."[24]

Another clue that can help detect a forged check is the absence of microprinting, an anticounterfeiting feature used in printing both checks and currency. Microprinting is the printing of text that is too small to be read by the naked eye.

Mailboxes with upright flags are obvious and easy targets for check washers.

On many checks today, microprinting can be found on the line signed by the account holder, and is marked with an MP. The microprinting looks like a solid black line. However, under a magnifying glass, it is obvious that there is no line—just words. On the other hand, if a counterfeiter creates checks with a printer or scanner, the line of microprinting will appear as a dotted line—and will alert the teller that the check is not legitimate.

Help from Witnesses

Sometimes forgers are caught in the early stages of the crime rather than at the end, when they are trying to cash the forged checks. Besides cashing the checks, forgers are most vulnerable when they are stealing account numbers. As with those who wash checks, check forgery rings steal outgoing mail in order to get the number of an account.

"Thieves drive around all day long stealing mail," says Kincaid. "They fill up their cars, hoping that some of those envelopes contain checks or even just account information, such as a bank statement."[25]

One ring of check forgers was eventually arrested after a woman noticed suspicious activity on her block in a suburb of Miami. She saw a car stop in front of her neighbor's house and watched as two women got out and took mail out of the mailbox. The women walked on to the next house and did the same thing. The car crawled behind them, and when their arms were full, they dumped the letters in the back seat. The witness reported the license plate to police, and they arrested a number of check counterfeiters.

Fingerprints on a Check

A final method of catching forgers is the use of forensic technology. Police crime labs are not used routinely in cases of check fraud, for the labs' top priority is solving violent crimes. "No matter what people see on TV," says Lt. Kincaid, "we don't look for DNA evidence for every crime."[26]

However, there are cases in which a great deal of money is being lost because tellers or retail clerks have not been able to spot the counterfeit checks in time to alert police. As the losses mount, investigators sometimes look for forensic clues to help them make an arrest.

Occasionally, fingerprint technicians can provide information crucial to the investigation, though on a porous surface such as paper or cardboard, fingerprints are latent—they cannot be seen with the naked eye. Even so, crime lab technicians have a number of ways to find them. One of the most common ways to retrieve prints from a check is to spray it with a chemical called ninhydrin. After spraying the check, technicians place it in a microwave oven. The heat develops the prints, turning them a vivid purple.

Cooperation Is the Key

Even the clearest fingerprints are worthless, however, unless an investigator can compare them with the prints of a suspect. Technicians may first compare the prints with those retrieved from any other counterfeit checks. If that does not produce a

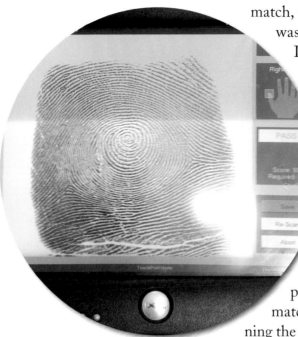

With IAFIS, a single fingerprint can sometimes lead to suspected forgers.

match, they use a computerized system that was developed in the 1980s called the Integrated Automated Fingerprint Identification System, or IAFIS. The system can scan the print and compare it with millions of other prints on file in minutes.

Sometimes fingerprints can help put an entire check ring out of business. One investigator noticed that several counterfeit checks passed in his area of eastern Missouri contained similar misspellings of Missouri cities. He processed the checks and found a matching print on all of them. After running the print through the IAFIS database, he was able to get a match and a name, and a suspect was taken into custody. The suspect readily gave up names of other members of the check forgery ring. "Sometimes it all works together," says a forensic lab technician. "And we on the lab side are gratified when we get to provide information that helps the investigators make an arrest. That's the best part of the job."[27]

"It's Really a War"

The investigation of check forgery is an ongoing challenge, however. No matter how careful and alert tellers and retail clerks are, no matter how many advances in antiforgery technology are developed, the numbers of forgers do not seem to lessen. "It's really a war," says Colliander. "Just when we think we are making progress, the crooks are ahead of us again. It's a question of staying vigilant, keeping our eyes open, and communicating with one another. For now, that's the best we can do."[28]

CHAPTER 2

Art Forgery

Checks are not the only targets of forgers. Long before there were banks, art forgers were hard at work—creating copies of the paintings and sculptures of others and selling them for profit. The ancient Romans, for example, were a military power but lacked a thriving artistic culture. Instead, Roman art forgers created copies of Greek sculpture and painting. So prevalent were such forgeries, in fact, that the first century B.C. satirist Horace observed, "He who knows a thousand works of art, knows a thousand frauds."[29]

"They're Stuffed Shirts"

There is more money to be made forging art today than ever before. Some collectors are willing to pay tens of millions of dollars for paintings by well-known artists such as Vincent van Gogh or Pablo Picasso. Some experts believe that as many as 20 percent of van Gogh paintings in circulation today may be fake—including the painting *Sunflowers*, which was purchased in 1987 by a Japanese company for almost $40 million.

Individual collectors are not the only ones being fooled. Thomas Hoving, a former director of the Metropolitan Museum of Art in New York, says that museums are often victims of forgers. Part of the problem, he maintains, is that the forensic analysis needed for authenticating a doubtful painting can be very expensive. More important, Hoving believes, is that it is embarrassing—especially for certain museum curators—to have to admit that they were fooled by an imitation. "They're stuffed shirts," he explains, "and they get hugely embarrassed."[30]

Even so, most art lovers want to know that the painting they are admiring is really the work of Rembrandt, or van Gogh, or Leonardo da Vinci. "It makes all the difference in the world to me," says art lover Terry Zech, who visited the Louvre museum in Paris just to see da Vinci's *Mona Lisa.* "Knowing I was standing there looking at something real, something Leonardo da Vinci painted five hundred years ago—it was magical. If I even had a doubt that it had been forged by some really talented art student, my experience wouldn't have been the same."[31]

One London art investigator agrees, saying that art forgers need to be exposed precisely for that reason—they are cheating the art lover out of that very experience—all for greed. For

St. George and the Dragon *hangs in London's National Gallery. Many experts think the painting is a forgery.*

the forger, he says, art is merely "a commodity—a means of making money for criminals."[32]

A Cotton-Candy Version of a Warhorse

The authenticity of a piece of art can be evaluated in a number of ways. Often, if there is any doubt as to whether the piece is a forgery, an art connoisseur may be consulted. A connoisseur is someone who is very familiar with the technique and work of a particular artist. A connoisseur viewing a painting that is said to be the work of van Gogh, for example, would be quick to note something that seemed a bit off, or unlike van Gogh's other work.

Thomas Hoving has had those very feelings about a painting hanging in the National Gallery in London—a painting he and several other connoisseurs are convinced is a forgery. It is called *St. George and the Dragon*, and it is supposed to have been painted by an Italian artist named Paolo Uccello during the fifteenth century. However, says Hoving, the painting lacks the strengths for which Uccello—whose other works show soldiers in armor on horseback—is famous. "The feeling of the *St. George* [painting] is quiet, detached, cautious—and dead," says Hoving. "The warrior's anatomy is fumbled. He has virtually no waist at all. The horse is a cotton-candy version of the marvelous steeds [in other Uccello paintings]."[33]

Not Scientific, but Useful

Hoving says that a portrait of Mark Twain supposedly painted by Swedish artist Anders Zorn looks equally suspicious to connoisseurs. Zorn was known for taking time to get the skin tones of his subjects to look especially realistic. The Twain portrait, however, "looks as if it had been painted too swiftly—as if it had emerged from a blender,"[34] according to Hoving.

Sometimes, it is not the lack of skill or artistry in a painting that a connoisseur notices, but a variance in technique.

"Sometimes it's just the way an artist does shading, or perspective," says one art history graduate student. "Especially in paintings done in oils, you see the evidence of the artist's brushstrokes. Artists have different ways they apply the paint. Does the painting show long, broad strokes, or short stuttery ones? Looking at the lines of the brush strokes visible on the paint, you can usually see a lot of consistency in an artist's work from one painting to another."[35]

The evaluations of connoisseurs are by no means scientific, and rarely is a piece of art deemed a forgery based on an art expert's analysis alone. There are, after all, a number of feasible explanations for inconsistency in skill or technique in an artist's work. The contrast may be due to an artist trying a different style or subject area. It could be because the two contrasting works are from different periods in the artist's life. Age or illness could account for noticeable differences in skill or technique, too.

Even so, a negative evaluation by a connoisseur is often enough to indicate that further analysis should be done on the work of art. Using a number of scientific instruments, investigators can provide a more exact analysis of the work that can show whether it is legitimate.

Checking Out the Canvas

When asked to provide an analysis of a painting, art investigators almost always begin by looking carefully at the canvas itself. Until 1830, canvases used by artists were woven by hand from linen. From 1830 on, canvases were woven on looms. By looking at the weave (no magnification is necessary), a forensic investigator can tell whether the canvas pre-dates 1830. If there are flaws in the canvas, such as rough spots or fibers of different sizes, it is obvious that the canvas was handmade.

The fibers used in the canvas can tell a story, too. Modern canvases can be made either of linen, in the older style, or of synthetic fabrics. By looking at samples of the threads on a canvas, an investigator can tell by the shape and formation of the

fibers which they are. Forensic investigator Walter McCrone once examined a Russian painting which was supposedly done in the 1700s.

"I tugged a few fibers from the cloth backing and put them under the microscope," McCrone recalls. "In cross section the fibers were cylindrical, a feature typical of man-made fabrics." A closer scrutiny of the fibers told him exactly what fabric. "The work had been painted on Dacron, a form of polyester that was not available until after 1953."[36] That told him instantly that the painting could not have been painted in the eighteenth century.

Circles of Wood

Not all paintings are done on canvas. Many artists have used wood paneling instead. An examination of the wood can provide even more information about the age of the painting than canvas. Scientists often rely on a process called dendrochronology, the science of establishing age based on the annual growth rings on trees.

This Salvador Dali exhibit, held in Finland in 2004, closed early after art collectors complained that the exhibit included hundreds of fakes.

"Money-Grubbing Confidence Men"

Art expert Thomas Hoving dispels a myth that art forgery is a victim-less crime, and that forgers are basically misunderstood.

Where do art forgers come from and who are they? Most will tell you that they aren't crooks, but deft, witty, jolly good fellows who intend no harm and who only create fakes as practical jokes. But these are few. The history of art forgery is crammed with self-proclaimed, to-be-pitied characters who claim they had to turn to fakery because the insidious art world spurned their genuinely creative efforts. And it is populated by miscreants who say they fake only to show up how stupid, blind, and pompous the art establishment is. Both justifications are as phony as the works they have fobbed on the world of art. Money is the root motive of art forgery. Most forgers are money-grubbing confidence men, delighted to cobble up something that will get by in the rush for big profits at little expense.

An artist making a small copy shows how easy it is to create a forgery.

Thomas Hoving, *False Impressions: The Hunt for Big-Time Art Fakes.* New York, Simon and Schuster, 1996, p. 22.

Every year in the life of a tree is marked by a ring on the trunk, visible when it is cut down. By counting the circles, one can establish the age of the tree—and therefore the age of the wood products made from that tree.

The scientist first identifies the type of wood used in the panel—usually beech, maple, poplar, or oak. The sides and back of the panel are gently swabbed to clean them, and the investigator can then look for a pattern of growth rings. Usually, dendrochronologists require an area of at least one hundred rings to be able to get the information they need.

With a magnifying glass, the scientist uses a special instrument that can measure the width of each ring down to a tenth of a millimeter. The widths of rings are crucial, for they reflect the amount of rain in a particular year. During a rainy year, trees grow very wide rings, while during dry years, the rings are narrow.

After measuring and counting the rings on the sample, the scientist enters the information into an extensive computer database containing the known tree ring patterns throughout Eastern and Western Europe through the centuries. The computer searches for that pattern matching the rings in question, and finally presents an accurate match.

Sometimes the process has happier results than proving a forgery. Dendrochronologist Peter Klein was asked to verify the date of an oak panel upon which a portrait had been painted. The owner of the painting believed the work was done in 1603. When Klein measured the ring sample from the panel, the computer database showed a match with a pattern of rings for an oak tree that dated back to 1323.

After counting 264 growth rings and adding the years wood was seasoned before being made into furniture and panels for painters, he estimated that the year 1603 for the painting seemed just right—an evaluation that relieved the painting's owner, who was worried that the portrait might have been a forgery.

Looking Beneath the Art

If after these examinations investigators have not found anything that raises suspicions that the work is a forgery, they continue to the next step—a look beneath the art. One of the forger's techniques is to fool examiners by painting over an old painting, reusing the canvas. It is impossible to see layers under the painting with the naked eye, so investigators use another method.

X-rays, the same alternate source of radiation used by doctors to view bones in the body, can be used to take photographs

Experts at the Prado Museum in Spain proved that The Milkmaid of Bordeaux *(pictured) was a forgery.*

of the canvas. Because different colors of paint absorb light X-rays differently, the X-ray photograph can provide a vivid image of any paint or ink underneath.

Of course, the presence of a painting underneath is not always an indication of forgery. Some artists are well known for recycling their old canvases and painting over a work they were dissatisfied with. But unless the painting underneath can be matched to the same artist as the one on the surface, it would be very suspicious to an investigator.

For instance, in 2001 art experts at the Prado, a famous museum in Madrid, Spain, wanted to check beneath the surface of a painting supposedly by Francisco de Goya. The painting, called *The Milkmaid of Bordeaux*, had connoisseurs puzzled, because it did not seem to be as good as most of Goya's other work. An X-ray showed that there was a sketch underneath the painting, and that immediately confirmed the fears of the museum staff. Said one expert, "Goya never did drawings underneath his paintings."[37] The painting was removed from the museum at once.

This sculpture of an Egyptian cat was determined to be a forgery in 1987, after experts compared it with another cat in the Metropolitan Museum's collection.

Paint is not the only evidence of forgery found by X-ray. One three-paneled painting, called a triptych, was thought to be a beautiful example of fifteenth-century Italian art. Within the three frames, however, X-ray photography showed the presence of machine-made nails and hinges—not possible in the fifteenth century.

Paints and Pigments

The final testing of most paintings is the analysis of the paint itself. Oil paints are made of pigments—some substance or combination of substances that provide color—and a medi-

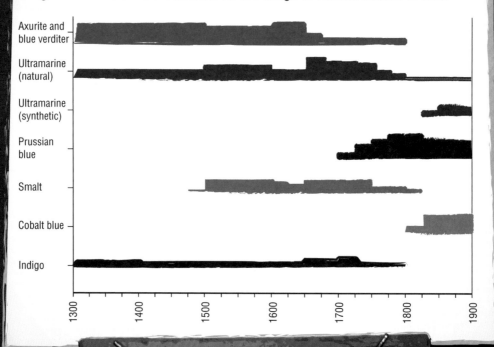

Detecting Forgery Through Paint Pigments

The most obvious method that fraud specialists use to expose art forgeries is by analyzing paint pigments. Since the various shades of color have changed over time, a chemical analysis of the paint can usually help to determine what era it originated in. Below is the timeline for the usage of various shades of blue.

um that thins the pigment to the right consistency. The pigments can provide valuable clues about a painting's authenticity to investigators.

When oil painting began in the fifteenth century, artists looked for bright, vivid pigments for their work. Each new pigment was documented as it was introduced over the years, and as a result of this documentation, investigators have an accurate timeline of their appearance. Any painting under investigation can be dismissed as a forgery if it contains pigments that are too recent to have been used at the time. Prussian blue, for example, was first created in 1704 and therefore could never have appeared in painting done by Rembrandt, who died in 1669.

The Secret of Chrome Yellow

One bright color that has tripped up more than one forger is called chrome yellow. It was widely used until the mid-1800s, when people noticed that air pollution from coal-burning homes and factories turned the color almost black. In 1975 chrome yellow made a comeback, however, but with an important improvement. The new chrome yellow pigment has particles that are coated with an element that keeps out pollution, so the color stays true.

Experts say this information is valuable for scientists trying to date a painting in which chrome yellow paint was used. By looking at a sample of the paint under a microscope, examiners can see whether the protective coating is present. If the painting is supposed to have been done before 1975, it can quickly be dismissed as a forgery. "It is small details like this," says forensic chemist Owen Facey, "which are not well publicized, that make it so difficult [for forgers] to reproduce exactly the materials from past years, even when they appear . . . to be the same."[38]

Microscopic Analysis

Any forensic examiner who must examine paint samples relies on at least two sorts of microscopes. The first is called a stereobinocular microscope. It is similar to a pair of magnifying goggles that can be attached to a movable arm that allows the scope to be moved across the surface of even the largest painting.

Using the microscope, the examiner finds spots on the painting from which to draw samples. Very fine needles are used in taking a bit of paint from the work. It is important not to do any obvious damage to the painting, so samples are taken from inconspicuous areas such as inside tiny cracks on the painting or from the edge of the canvas under the frame. Only a tiny sample is necessary—no bigger than a speck of sand for each color that needs examination.

Once the samples are gathered, the examiner puts the sample on a slide and views it under a polarized light microscope. This is a special instrument that can identify all individual particles that make up each pigment. If a pigment shows up on a painting where it should not, say experts, that is all the proof necessary to discredit it.

Prints in the Paint

Scientists can use that same stereoscopic microscope to search old paintings for a very modern forensic clue—fingerprints. Artists have often used their fingers to smooth out areas of paint or to achieve an effect that was impossible with a brush. Occasionally, too, an artist might accidentally leave prints on a painting. If a print is found, it can provide information about who the artist was, or was not.

Unlike latent prints, which are invisible except under certain light sources, fingerprints in a substance such as blood or paint are visible, or patent. They show the tiny ridges on the tips of one's fingers that form a pattern unique to that individual. When the investigator finds a print, it is photographed so that it can later be studied in the laboratory.

Of course, fingerprinting was not known as a forensic tool before the twentieth century, so prints of artists like da Vinci and Rembrandt are not available. However, forensic examiners looking at a painting purporting to be a da Vinci, for example, can use their microscope on other da Vinci paintings

Making Wavelets

 New methods of detecting art forgery are always being investigated. Some are grounded in forensic science, others in establishing a work's provenance. One promising new method actually attempts to measure the art itself, rather than paint, canvas, and other features.

Computer technicians take a painting and, using four powerful computers, scan it digitally. They then convert the scans into mathematical images that can be seen as a series of peaks and valleys, and various wavelengths. Called wavelet analysis, it is based on the idea that a painter's individual techniques result in similar wavelet patterns on a computer, no matter what the subject of the painting. By comparing the wavelet pattern to a pattern scanned from a known work by the same painter, technicians should be able to authenticate an unknown work.

This is especially helpful in assessing abstract works, such as paintings by Jackson Pollock—art that seems to have no pattern at all. Though wavelet analysis is in its early stages, many art authenticators see its promise for the future.

Modern technology has opened many doors in preventing art forgeries from passing as authentic works.

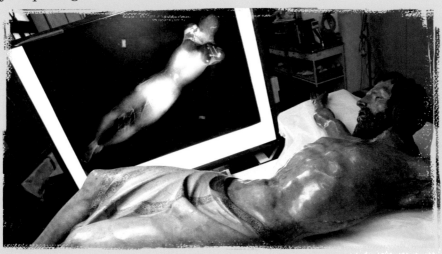

in museums around the world. If a matching print is found on a known da Vinci, the chances are good that the questioned painting is legitimate.

The Biography of a Work of Art

Examinations by connoisseurs and forensic scientists are not the only important steps in uncovering a forgery. Historians play an extremely valuable role in verifying the history, or provenance, of a piece of art. The provenance is like the work's biography, providing information on when the work was created, as well as who owned it, sold it, or donated it—and when.

Often the provenance can be traced in deeds, bills of sale, wills, and other documents. Other times, information about the work can be found in letters from the artist to friends or family members. Van Gogh, for example, wrote many letters to his brother Theo, describing in great detail the paintings and drawings he was working on. Some of these letters have helped historians place particular paintings in a chronology, or timetable, of the artist's other work. That creates a starting place in filling in the rest of the painting's biography.

The provenance of a work of art is so important that many museums and dealers refuse to even consider the authenticity of a painting if it has no history. What art experts hope to see, writes reporter Doris Athineos, is the clear evidence of a paper trail:

> Like stickers on a steamer trunk, labels stuck on a painting's backside chronicle its trip through galleries, museums, and private collections. As the work winds its way through the museum circuit on exhibit, it also earns letters and clips from critics, art historians, and curators. This documentation confers status and authenticity, and gives collectors confidence to pay big bucks."[39]

The Power of Provenances

Knowing the importance of provenances, however, crooks have sometimes forged them, too. In fact, one English painter created forgeries that could never have stood up under scientific examination, but whose documents were so well-forged that for years no one suspected the paintings were not legitimate.

John Myatt forged more than two hundred paintings by great artists such as van Gogh and Picasso, and all the while his business partner, John Drewe, was forging fake provenances. Drewe used antique typewriters to create old-looking letters and bills of sale. He acquired stationery or forms used by dealers and filled them in himself. Drewe even gained access to the archives of large museums and

By the Numbers

2,000

Number of fake Renoirs and Rembrandts created by English forger Thomas Keating.

planted such documents in their files and inserted photos of the paintings in old exhibition catalogs—signifying that the work had been shown on those occasions. In addition, he used names of art dealers that had since gone out of business, so it would be harder for buyers or dealers to verify the information. Few dealers had the time or inclination to check what appeared to be real documents, and Myatt's paintings continued to sell.

The Tate Gallery in London (pictured) was a victim of provenance forger John Drewe.

Remarkably, even though the quality of Myatt's work was not great, dealers say that they believed the paintings were real because their provenances were on file in some of the finest museums. "You go to the Tate Gallery archives," says one expert, "and you look through the stock book of the most reputable gallery in London in the fifties, and you find the picture reproduced in black and white. You can't be more diligent than that."[40]

The fraud was revealed when Drewe's girlfriend went to the police and told them about documents she found that seemed illegal. Scientific tests were then carried out on some of Myatt's paintings and not surprisingly proved they were forgeries. Drewe, considered the mastermind of the fraud, was sentenced to six years in prison, and Myatt to twelve months.

"Much Harder to Come By"

Art investigators say that it takes only one bit of evidence, such as a too-modern canvas or a paint pigment that was not available during the lifetime of the artist, to prove forgery. However, it is far more difficult to prove that a work of art is legitimate. "Proof of authenticity," admits forensic expert McCrone, "is much harder to come by."[41]

A forger could use the correct paints and canvas and execute the painting with skill that might fool even the most knowledgeable connoisseur. It would be very hard to prove that the painting was forged. If art experts are correct in their view that a great deal of the art pieces in circulation today are forged, the forensic world may need to develop more accurate tools by which to evaluate them.

Paper, Ink, and Penmanship

While some forgers attempt to get rich by faking paintings and other works of art, others apply their criminal talents to forging written documents. Some create phony wills, while others pen bogus letters and other historical memorabilia. Forgers take advantage of the fact that autographs and handwritten documents can demand extraordinarily high prices among collectors.

A $748,000 Autograph

Dealers in rare documents charge tens of thousands of dollars for authentic signatures by a variety of famous people. "Some people might think that the movie and television stars are the most sought-after signatures," says one collector, "but those aren't the ones that draw the most money. I've heard of someone buying a letter written by Abraham Lincoln, in which he defends the Emancipation Proclamation, for $748,000—and I think that was back in the early 1990s. Maybe by now there have even been higher priced ones."[42]

With so much money at stake, whether from a forged will or a note signed by Albert Einstein, it is crucial to determine that the document is authentic. If someone suspects a forgery, a questioned document (QD) examiner is asked to give an expert analysis. Just as with questioned works of art, investigators of questioned documents must first prove that a forgery has been committed. Once that has been shown, it is rarely difficult to find the guilty party. "Like most other crimes where money is involved," says one investigator, "with forgery, you ask yourself, 'Who benefits the most?' Most of the time, [finding the forger] is a pretty straightforward path, following the money."[43]

Looking at Handwriting

In the majority of QD cases, handwriting gives away the forgery. Everyone has his or her unique style, and someone trying to imitate that style without leaving obvious clues faces an extraordinarily difficult job. Merely being able to mimic the handwriting—the shape and form of the letters themselves—is not enough for a forger to fool QD examiners.

The first step for an examiner is to assemble as many samples of the person's handwriting as possible. He or she looks at letters, notes, and checks. QD examiners pay careful attention not only to how the subject writes alphabetical letters, but also

A witness identifies his signature in a case involving fraudulent absentee ballots.

at the way t's are crossed and i's are dotted, and how numbers are written. They also pay attention to whether a person tends to write uphill or on a straight line.

There are several key characteristics of most forged handwriting. One is called "forger's tremor"—shaky, tentative handwriting that results from slow, methodical copying. The forger starts and stops and lifts the pen off the paper as he or she checks the writing against the document being forged. Using a magnifying glass, the experienced examiner can clearly identify such pauses and starts in the marks of the pen.

A Suspicious Will

Forger's tremor was one of the clues found by QD examiners who were asked to verify a will by the billionaire recluse Howard Hughes. After Hughes died in 1976, a will that had not been seen before mysteriously turned up. According to this will, Hughes left one-sixteenth of his estate to a Nevada gas station owner named Melvin Dummar. Seemingly astounded by his good fortune, Dummar recalled picking up a hitchhiker in the desert—an old man who he said might have been Hughes.

An FBI document specialist who was asked to examine the will later recalled that the handwritten will contained so many examples of forger's tremor that he had no doubt that it was bogus: "The Hughes will was full of those things I would expect to see in a simulated forgery: blunt endings, retouches as the forger attempted to correct mistakes, illogical stopping places where the forger had to go back and look at the model he was copying, very poor line quality. It was a bad job."[44]

The findings were presented to Dummar, and he eventually admitted that he had made up the story and forged the will.

A Forged Franklin Signature

On the other hand, shaky writing sometimes can prove a document to be authentic. Age or illness can affect handwriting, and some forgers have forgotten this—and their forgery was discovered as a result.

Joseph Cosey, one of the most talented forgers in U.S. history, was skilled at replicating the signatures of many historical figures, especially those who lived in the eighteenth century. When Cosey forged a pay warrant from 1787 signed by Benjamin Franklin, he did not take into account that Franklin's handwriting had changed significantly in his old age.

The date Cosey put on the pay warrant was three years before Franklin's death at age eighty-four—unusually old for those days—and his authentic signatures show shakiness and difficulty forming the capital letter F. The forgery, however, showed handwriting as strong as in Franklin's youth.

Charles Hamilton, one of the most famous handwriting experts in the world, was familiar with the work of Cosey and said that while the counterfeit documents he produced were excellent, Cosey tended to make one particular error: "[W]hether Cosey writes an early or late Franklin document, he never varies the handwriting. His scribbling Franklin is timeless, an eternal youth whose handsome script remained firm and bold to the very end."[45]

Too Perfect

Ironically, while many forgeries are discovered because the handwriting differs from authentic samples of the subject, there have been cases solved because the forgery was too perfect. Handwriting experts say that it is extremely rare for anyone to sign his or her name twice in exactly the same way.

"Every individual's handwriting is unique. Even you can't write your own name precisely the same way twice," challenges forensic researcher David Fisher. "Write your signature on two separate pieces of paper, then lay one over the other and hold them up to a light. They will be close, but one will never exactly cover the other."[46]

Another fake will of a wealthy man was forged by someone who did not realize this fact. Each page of a will is signed by the person it belongs to, as a way of testifying that the material in each section is accurate. In the will of millionaire W.M. Rice, the signatures on each of the four pages matched perfectly—too perfectly, according to QD examiners. They believed that someone had traced Rice's signature on each page of the will.

The examiners studied samples of Rice's signature from the weeks before his death, and those showed the small variances that are normal. On the basis of the four perfect signatures, the will was eventually declared a forgery. It turned out that a greedy lawyer not only forged the document but also murdered the eighty-four-year-old Rice to get the money more quickly.

The Shrinking Signature

Two other aspects of handwriting forgery experts look for are the size and alignment of a signature. For some reason, most forgers—even very skilled ones—write a signature noticeably smaller than it should be. Handwriting expert Hamilton feels that writing smaller shows "the forger's unconscious tenden-

Signature Red Flags

Handwriting analysts like Charles Hamiliton know there are important signs of a forgery that may be obvious not only in the handwriting of a signature but in the name that the subject signed. A knowledge of history and a familiarity with other documents that person has signed can help a collector judge whether the signature is authentic.

Founding father Patrick Henry, for example, signed everything only with the initial of his first name. Abraham Lincoln, on the other hand, had a variety of signatures, depending on the occasion. He used "A. Lincoln" as a signature on letters, and on official documents he always signed "Abraham Lincoln." Personal letters to friends of family were usually signed "Lincoln." He never used "Abe" for anything. A dealer offering for sale a Lincoln letter signed in a way that differs from these, say experts, should not get a collector's business.

Signatures differ in the way people form specific letters which make them hard to forge well.

cy to shrink the size of his subject's handwriting—probably because of a psychological desire to conceal his fraud by making it less easy to read."[47] Other experts feel that there may be another reason, too. They point out that a number of forgers copy signatures they have seen in books or magazines, and those signatures may not be printed to scale. As a result, the forger may not realize the size of the subject's real signature.

One example is the highly sought-after signature of George Washington. The most talented Washington forger was Robert Spring, who lived in the nineteenth century. Though Washington's signatures tended to be 3 inches (7.6 cm) long, Spring's forgeries were about two-thirds that size. Forgers making money from former president Richard M. Nixon's signature make the same mistake. Nixon's signature was usually a 4-inch-long (10.2 cm) sprawl, while fakes are about half that length.

A letter in the hand of Queen Elizabeth I and a note in the hand of Shakespeare both turned out to be forgeries perpetrated by W. H. Ireland.

Paper Clues

It is not only handwriting, however, that can give away a forgery. QD examiners also look carefully at the paper used, especially

in historical documents. Just as the examination of an artist's canvas can help experts establish a date for a painting, a sheet of paper can provide the same type of information.

Sometimes examiners chemically test the paper. Paper has changed a great deal through the centuries, especially in the ingredients used to produce it. Some papers are made from grass, others from linen or wood pulp. These ingredients can be seen under a microscope.

Document examiners also pay very close attention to any chemicals that have been added. By knowing when paper mills began using certain chemicals for whitening, for example, an investigator may narrow the date of when the document was written.

However, experts say that determining that the paper was two hundred years old, for example, does not always mean that document itself is that old. Many a skilled forger has taken an old book and torn out the flyleaf—the blank page at the beginning or end—and used it for creating an old document. William Henry Ireland, who forged a great number of documents purportedly written by William Shakespeare, admitted that he used such old paper to make his fakes look authentic. "I applied to a bookseller . . . who, for the sum of five shillings, suffered me to take from the . . . volumes in his shop the flyleaves which they contained."[48]

A Message in the Paper

A watermark is one very valuable tool in establishing the date of a piece of paper. Watermarks are emblems, dates, or other images impressed into the paper during its manufacture. A watermark usually identifies the papermaker, but throughout history some buyers have requested their own unique watermark.

George Washington, for example, had a watermark on his presidential stationery with an image of Lady Liberty sitting on a plow.

An examiner gets the best look at a watermark when a light box is used. This is a shallow wooden box with an opaque glass top over a flat light source. When a document is placed on it, light bulbs inside the box illuminate the document from behind, showing the watermark in great detail. Some of the watermarks have dates, which help immensely. The U.S. Secret Service has a historical collection of more than twenty-two thousand different watermarks as well as the years during which they were used.

Foolish Errors

Several forgeries were thwarted because of a crook's ignorance or carelessness about watermarks. One was a very well-written fake of President John F. Kennedy's famous quote from his inaugural address: "Ask not what your country can do for you, ask what you can do for your country." The forger had somehow obtained a sheet of White House stationery and had done an impressive job of writing the famous words as well as JFK's difficult signature.

However, expert Kenneth Rendell notes, he did not notice that the stationery bore a watermark of 1981, which was eighteen years after Kennedy was assassinated. "The skill of the forger," says Rendell, "did not extend to the common sense of holding the blank piece of White House stationery up to the light."[49]

Another crime was averted when QD examiners were asked to investigate a will supposedly discovered in a trunk belonging to the man who had died. The will was dated 1912 and had a watermark indicating the paper was made by the Berkshire Bond company. By checking with Berkshire officials, the examiners found that the particular stationery was not made until 1916. The relative named in the will was charged with forgery.

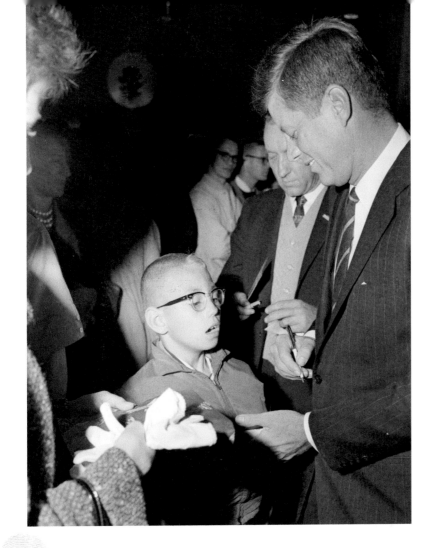

John F. Kennedy pauses for autographs. Watermarks foiled a skillful forgery of the former president's signature on a letter.

Evaluation of Ink

Like paper, ink can be examined for clues of forgery. While all black ink may look the same, for example, there are many differences in the chemical makeup of each type of black ink. The ingredients have changed through the centuries, and investigators can perform tests on a sample of ink from a questioned document that can reveal when it was used. If the ink is too modern to be on a particular document, that proves that the piece is not authentic.

Ink from the seventeenth and eighteenth centuries was made of a number of natural or synthetic ingredients. Through the years, however, manufacturers have added ingredients that improve the color or permanence of the ink. Since 1969 ink makers have included chemical compounds that are like identification tags. By knowing the year one of these compounds was added to ink, examiners can be accurate about establishing a date for a QD.

Migrating Ink

A process called thin-layer chromatography enables examiners to identify the chemical ingredients in an ink sample. First, the examiner takes a very thin, hollow needle and punches it through an inked part of the document. This tiny bit of paper is put in a test tube along with a special substance called a solvent, which turns the ink back into a liquid.

Once the ink has dissolved, a drop of the solvent/ink mixture is placed on a paper strip. Other samples of known inks

Typewriter Analysis

A great number of forgeries are a combination of typed text and a signature. Though typewriters are rarely used today, they were common in offices and homes throughout most of the twentieth century. Each brand of typewriter had a somewhat different sort of type. As a result, law enforcement technicians could look closely at a typed letter or note, and by comparing it to samples of various machines, could almost always tell what brand of typewriter it had been written on, as well as when it was written.

This fact has allowed document examiners to identify a large number of forgeries. One that makes experts laugh was a message supposedly typed and signed by Albert Einstein. The message was his famous equation: $E = mc^2$. However, the type was quickly matched to a modern IBM typewriter that was not used until six years after Einstein's death.

are placed on the strip, too. Then the strip is dipped into another solvent that slowly soaks into the paper, dragging the various inks along with it. The examiners look carefully at the way each sample breaks down into smaller areas that travel different distances on the strip.

Once the inks stop migrating, the patterns of movement are measured and compared to a database of more than three thousand ink chromatograph patterns. Using this information, examiners can identify the various chemical components of the ink.

Outfoxing a Smart Forger

Ink can also trip up a forger who uses a flyleaf from an old book for creating a manuscript. Experts say that as paper ages, it becomes more and more absorbent. That means that ink used on very old paper will be absorbed rapidly, spreading into a feathery pattern that is often obvious even without a magnifying glass or microscope. "It's like writing with a marker on a paper towel," says one forensic technician. "The ink just kind of blossoms out."[50]

Hundreds of attempted forgeries have been foiled this way—from a phony copy of Lincoln's Gettysburg Address to signatures of Thomas Jefferson and John Adams. In each case the writing was misshapen and odd-looking from the feathering, either to the naked eye or under a microscope. And in each case examiners were able to quickly give their verdict: forgery.

"Have a Nice Day"

In addition to the varied scientific tests and the use of microscopes and other instruments to expose forged documents, a knowledge of history is of great value, too. In fact, in many cases the expense and trouble of performing lengthy laboratory examinations can be avoided if an investigator knows something about the times of the individual who was supposedly the author of the QD. Sometimes the forger's mistakes are less about the paper, ink, and handwriting than they are about what he or she has written in the fake document.

George Washington's famous signature, shown here, has been the subject of many forgery attempts.

A letter signed by George Washington is a case in point. The letter closed with the words "Yours truly" before the signature—a common closing phrase most people are familiar with. However, in George Washington's day that phrase was almost never used—especially in an official letter. The word choice alone marked the document as a fake. One document examiner says sarcastically, "The forger of the Washington letter might as well have written . . . "Have a Nice Day, [signed] George."[51]

Another such mistake was a well-written pay authorization by Benjamin Franklin, signed on October 4, 1786. The authorization is made to Silas Hill, "being due him for services and attendance as a member of Congress."[52] An experienced investigator eventually discovered the forgery by checking on the political career of Silas Hill. He found that no one by that name had ever been a member of Congress.

"Almost Every Historical Blunder"

The love letters supposedly sent between Abraham Lincoln and a young woman named Ann Rutledge are another example of QDs exposed as forgeries because of their content. According to historians, there has never been sufficient evidence that the two were linked romantically. Whether or not young Lincoln was in love with Rutledge, however, document examiners say that the letters are clearly forgeries. According to expert Charles Hamilton, "The forged exchange of letters . . . discloses almost every historical blunder it is possible for a forger to commit."[53]

One of the most obvious blunders is the way Lincoln signs his name Abe. Historians have always been aware that he detested the nickname, and never signed any of his other correspondence in that manner.

Abraham Lincoln is said to have met Ann Rutledge in this tavern.

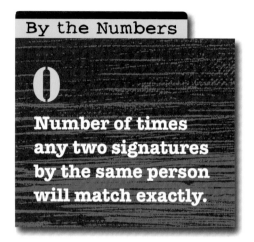

Another mistake the forger made is in the grammar and spelling of the letters. Lincoln was known to have prided himself, even as a young man, on his mastery of the English language and its rules. The love letters, however, made him sound almost illiterate. He supposedly writes: "There is only five letters. If they keep the postage up to 25 cts for each letter poor poeple cannot avail themselves much . . . however I am going over to Grahams as he is going to help me in my grammer."[54]

The letters purportedly from Ann are even worse:

"I am trying to do as you ask me to praktise . . . if you git me the dictshinery . . . I no I can do both speeking and riting better. I am glad you sed that girls aint supposed to no like boys . . . my hart runs over with hapyness when I think yore name."[55]

As with many forgeries of historical documents, the identity of the forger is not known for certain. However, says one collector, it is enough just for people to know when a document is not authentic:

There's no doubt that forgeries can result in the loss of money and great disappointment for those who believed they had some exciting piece of history in their possession. . . . But by exposing [the forgeries], it's possible to stop the chain of fraud, so dealers and private collectors don't keep recycling documents that are fakes. Really, a lot of the forgeries out there were done by people that are dead by now. Identifying their work is probably the best way to resolve a crime like this.[56]

CHAPTER 4

Two Expensive Forgeries

While many forgers of historical documents do so to make money from selling them to collectors or dealers, there have been two large, highly publicized forgeries in recent years that were carried out on a much grander scale. One was a diary, the other a supposed autobiography of a famous person, and both were sold not to private collectors, but to large publishing houses for enormous amounts of money. Both forgeries were also exposed not by one single clue, but by a combination of scientific technology and investigative research.

"The Most Audacious Forger"

Clifford Irving became a household name in 1971 when McGraw-Hill publishers announced that the forty-one-year-old author was assisting the billionaire recluse Howard Hughes in writing his autobiography. In truth, however, Irving was forging the entire manuscript—and his publishers had no idea that they were being swindled out of more than $750,000.

QD experts rank Irving as one of the most gutsy forgers who ever lived. This was no autograph or letter he was forging, but a 230,000-word manuscript about the details of the life of Howard Hughes. The fact that his subject was still alive made Irving's forgery even more amazing. Hamilton calls Irving's project "the most incredible feat performed by the most audacious forger of this or any century."[57]

Irving knew that his scheme could fall apart very easily. All that would have to happen would be Hughes publicly denouncing the book as a fraud—but Irving was banking that that would not happen. Hughes, who had been a noted inventor and financier, had not been seen in public for more than fifteen years.

A Man of Mystery

Hughes's disappearance from public life was what made the idea of his autobiography so appealing to the public, and of course, to the publisher, who would make millions of dollars from the book. "I remember it so well," says Charlie Johnson, who worked at a radio station in the 1960s.

Everybody in the media was following the story of this book. No one knew anything about what Howard Hughes was doing, but there were rumors all over the place.

Some people said he really had turned into kind of a zombie, with hair down to his shoulders. You heard things, like his fingernails were eight inches long and he never bathed. You heard that he had all kinds of phobias, and his staff was cleaning everything constantly because Hughes was scared of germs.

Clifford Irving fooled publisher McGraw-Hill into thinking he was helping billionaire Howard Hughes write his autobiography.

But there was no way of knowing whether any of this was true. I think people were so fascinated by a billionaire—for one thing—and that he was so intent on maintaining his privacy that he lived like a hermit. Who knows what was true—but when people were told there was this book in which Hughes told his life story, that was really, really big."[58]

What was not simply rumor, however, was that Hughes was adamant about not

being seen in public. He spent his time in Las Vegas, where he lived on the top floor of a hotel, or in a secluded retreat in the Bahamas. So private was he, in fact, that he forfeited millions of dollars by not appearing in court to protect his gambling licenses in Nevada. Irving believed that anyone who would be willing to lose that much money to remain out of the public eye would not be likely to come forward to debunk the forged autobiography he was writing.

Howard Hughes (center) participates in a parade in New York City in 1938. Hughes's fortune would be the center of many forgery schemes.

Forging Letters

Irving got the idea for the forgery after reading an article about Hughes in *Newsweek*. The article was accompanied by a photograph of one of Hughes's handwritten letters. Irving practiced the handwriting style and signature, then forged letters supposedly written by Hughes—all responses to fictitious letters from Irving.

In one, Hughes thanked Irving for sending him a copy of his most recent book. Another was Hughes's response to a suggestion that Irving might collaborate with him on an autobiography. Hughes wrote: "It would not suit me to die without having certain misconceptions cleared up and without having stated the truth about my life. The immorality you speak of does not interest me, not in this world. I believe in obligations. . . . I would be grateful if you would let me know when and how you wish to undertake the writing of the biography you proposed."[59]

Irving took the letters to his publisher, McGraw-Hill, and soon negotiated a deal in which Hughes would make $750,000, from which the billionaire would pay a share to Irving. In addition, Irving made deals with a magazine that wanted the serial rights, and with another publisher for paperback rights. It seemed that Irving's fraud was well on its way.

Excitement and Doubt

Irving began writing the book, getting most of his information from articles published about Howard Hughes before he became a recluse. He wrote about Hughes's early life, his pioneering as an aviator, and his experiences as a film producer. While the articles helped somewhat, Irving found far more helpful information in an unpublished manuscript written by Hughes's former accountant. Irving secretly made a copy of the manuscript and used a great deal of the information contained in it.

The editors at McGraw-Hill were delighted when Irving presented them with a thousand-page manuscript. They loved the details and anecdotes it contained and noted that it gave a rare glimpse of a very private man. Representatives of the publishing company proudly made a public announcement about the upcoming book in December 1971.

However, there were rumblings from business advisers of Howard Hughes. They claimed that Hughes would never have agreed to such a book and condemned Irving and the book deal as a fraud. Irving insisted that the book was legitimate and that Hughes's associates did not know what they were talking about. McGraw-Hill executives, however, worried that their future best seller was being derailed, wanted proof that Irving's project was real.

"Less than One in a Million"

Clifford Irving had shown his publishers the forged letters from Howard Hughes. They also had the contract with Hughes's forged signature. However, the publishers brought in a forensic handwriting specialist to examine the letters more carefully.

Newsman Mike Wallace talks with author Clifford Irving before a newscast.

Interestingly, the professional was fooled. He compared the forged letters with known samples of Hughes's handwriting, studying the angles and shapes of the letters as well as their size. Finally, he declared that the letters were genuine. "It can be stated," he said, "that the two handwriting specimens were written by the same person. The chances that another person could copy this handwriting even in a similar way are less than one in a million."[60] The project was back on track. With the positive analysis of the handwriting, it appeared that Irving's scheme would succeed—at least until the following week, when Howard Hughes broke his fifteen-year public silence.

John Meier, a former aide to Howard Hughes, talks with the press after testifying in the Hughes autobiography case.

"Clifford Irving Is a Phony"

On January 7, 1972, aides of Hughes arranged for a conference call to be held, in which the billionaire would speak by telephone with reporters. Seven reporters, together with sev-

Becoming a Document Analyst

Job Description:
A document analyst examines handwriting, as well as typed or computer-printed material. The analyst forms conclusions of the authenticity or likely authorship of written material based on scrutiny of handwriting characteristics, grammar, and word choices. The physical characteristics of ink and paper are also examined.

Education:
Most law enforcement agencies want a four-year degree in criminalistics, chemistry, biology, or forensic science. An analyst is almost always required to have a current Forensic Document Examiner Certificate from the American Board of Forensic Document Examination.

Qualifications:
Employers look for a person who is knowledgeable about inks and the databases used to identify them, paper, and other physical characteristics of documents.

Salary:
Document analysts earn between $28,500 and $60,000 per year, though some who do freelance work with other agencies may earn more.

eral Hughes associates, gathered in a large room in a Los Angeles hotel and listened as a man claiming to be Howard Hughes talked via telephone from the Bahamas. During the call, Hughes flatly denied that he was participating in any project with Clifford Irving. "The book is a phony, and Clifford Irving is a phony," he said. "I never met him and I never wrote any autobiography."[61]

Those in the room who had spoken with Hughes in the past were certain that it was he on the telephone. "That was Howard Hughes's voice," said one man who had known Hughes for years. "There's no question about it. A lot of people can imitate voices, but his mannerisms of speech, his halting manner, were unmistakable."[62]

Irving, however, continued to insist that the project was real and that he had talked more than one hundred times with Hughes about the book. Further, he maintained that there was no shred of evidence that the man on the telephone was Hughes. "I'd like to know when these guys last saw Howard Hughes," he said. "I'm betting that they haven't seen him in years."[63]

This telephone conference became controversial. If the caller was really Hughes, as most of those in the room during the conference believed, then the letters from Hughes had obviously been forged by Irving. The case rested on proving that the caller was Howard Hughes. Determining for certain whether or not the voice matched the billionaire Hughes was an opportunity for a new forensic tool to be used.

Using the Spectrograph

This instrument is known as a spectrograph and is capable of comparing samples of human voices to prove whether or not they are from the same person. Scientist Lawrence Kersta, who had developed the system which was 99.65 percent accurate in identification of voice matches, was asked to analyze the voice of the caller.

The spectrograph is based on the idea that everyone has slightly different sound to his or her voice. Some of the differences are obvious—how deep the voice is, whether it is nasal, the speed at which someone talks, and whether there is a noticeable accent. However, there are subtle differences, too, that cannot as easily be sensed by the ear alone. Vocal sounds come from the vocal cords but are affected by the tongue, the teeth, and the lips. The ways the voice is affected by any of these variables can be so small that they can be distinguished only by a sensitive instrument such as the spectrograph.

The instrument changes the sounds of the voice into electronic impulses, which can then be plotted on a grid. A computer changes the pattern into a visual graphic. This graphic is called a voiceprint and can be easily compared with another voiceprint to see if they came from the same person. Experts say that even if someone were to try to disguise the voice by speaking at a higher or lower pitch, the spectrograph is almost never fooled. It still shows the same pattern—just at a higher or lower location on the screen.

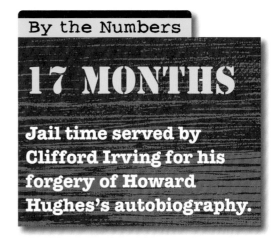

By the Numbers

17 MONTHS

Jail time served by Clifford Irving for his forgery of Howard Hughes's autobiography.

In this case, Kersta used a recording from 1947, when Hughes had testified before a U.S. Senate subcommittee. Though that recording had been made twenty-four years before, Kersta had no trouble in matching the two voiceprints. After studying the voiceprints, Kersta announced that the two matched: "The voices are so obviously the same that there's not much hesitation on my part in saying that, in my opinion, the voices in both cases are the same. I rarely say that I'm almost 100 percent convinced. But, in this case, I'm pretty close to 100 percent confident. . . . I'd say it's as close to 100 percent as I as a scientist would want to go."[64]

Following the Money

Coincidentally, other aspects of the investigation were proving equally damning to Irving. The hundreds of thousands of dollars paid to H.R. Hughes were missing, and if Hughes had not been paid, investigators wanted to know who had the money. In following the money trail, they found that the checks had been cashed in Switzerland—by a woman named H.R. Hughes.

Further digging found that Irving's wife, Edith, had a Swiss passport that had been falsified. Later, Irving admitted that he

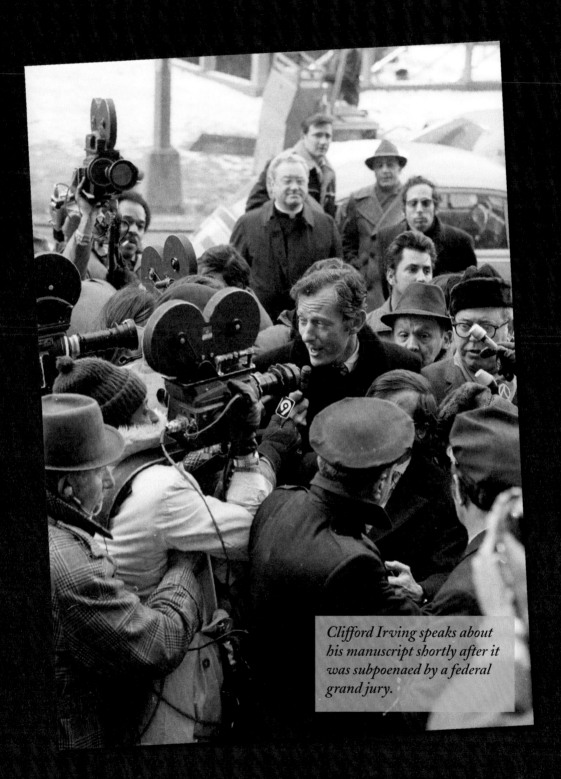

Clifford Irving speaks about his manuscript shortly after it was subpoenaed by a federal grand jury.

had changed the photograph in the passport, replacing it with one he took in which Edith was wearing a black wig. He also had erased her signature and had her sign her name as H.R. Hughes. In doing so, she had been able to access $750,000 in McGraw-Hill's check payments intended for Howard Hughes.

With the voiceprint and the forged passport, Irving knew he had no chance of continuing the fraud. He confessed, and was given a brief prison sentence. Ironically, after his release, Irving wrote a best-selling book about the forgery, called *The Hoax*.

An Amazing Discovery

Seven years later another controversial literary event caught the public's interest. This time it began in Europe, where editors at *Stern*, a West German weekly magazine, made an exciting announcement on April 22, 1983. Sixty-two volumes of Adolf Hitler's long-secret diaries had been discovered, and *Stern* had bought them—for about 9 million German marks, at that time equal to $3.8 million. The magazine planned to publish the diaries in what they described as "the journalistic scoop of the post–World War II period."[65]

In addition to scooping the rest of the world in publishing the diaries, *Stern* hoped to make millions more selling the rights to other magazines and newspapers around the world. They even had plans for a television documentary based on the diaries. After all, Adolf Hitler had been one of the most powerful Europeans who ever lived, and the public was definitely interested. "He was the worst of the dictators, the most despicable," says history teacher Katherine Spanish. "And that is probably why people have been fascinated with his life. What went on in his mind, how did he think? I remember quite well the talk about the diaries . . . and I was interested, just as millions of others around the world were, I expect."[66]

But within two weeks after the announcement, the diaries were found to be a forgery, and that discovery proved to be a costly mistake for those magazines and newspapers that had purchased serial rights. It was also an example of what can happen when greed overpowers common sense and actually helps the forger carry out the crime.

Early Doubts

At first, the discovery of diaries belonging to Hitler was not totally far-fetched. Historians know that Hitler, in the last days of the war, had airlifted his advisers as well as a trunk containing his private files before Berlin was seized by the Russian army. It was known, too, that the flight crashed soon after taking off and that everyone aboard was killed. Yet if the trunk had survived, many wondered, why had no one come forward with the diaries in the past thirty-eight years?

Stern correspondent Gerd Heidemann (right) discusses the Hitler diaries with reporters.

The fact that Hitler kept diary volumes was puzzling, too. He almost always dictated his thoughts to a secretary rather than doing the writing himself. In addition, Hitler's right hand had trembled from palsy, which would have made extensive writing difficult.

There were calls for *Stern* to authenticate the diaries, just in case they were forgeries. However, editors were reluctant, saying only "that their trusted correspondent, Gerd Heidemann . . . had acquired the priceless documents and that he would not disclose who gave them to him or who had hidden them for so many years."[67]

Even so, the editors agreed to allow some examination of the diaries. They sent a few of the volumes to the German Federal Archives for analysis—a process that would take some time to complete. *Stern* did not want to wait, however. The first extracts of the diaries were published by *Stern*, followed closely by the *London Times*, whose executives had purchased serial rights to the diaries. As one document examiner later recalled, "The opportunities for sensible research disappeared as *Stern* raced into print with its sensation."[68]

By the Numbers

60,000

Increase in circulation of *London Times* the week it published the forged Hitler Diaries.

"Real Leather or Nothing at All"

After the first installment of the diaries was published, more and more doubts arose, especially among historians. For some, the photographs of the sixty-two individual notebooks alone raised some questions about why Hitler would choose to write in notebooks of cheap imitation leather. "I have seen Hitler's fine leather desk set," said one document analyst, "and these leatherette notebooks did not resemble documents he would have left for posterity."[69]

Even a former colonel in Hitler's air force who had known the man well was more than skeptical. He emphatically denied that Hitler would ever have used such notebooks. "Artificial leather!" he snorted. "Hitler would have had real leather or nothing at all."[70]

The consistency of the diaries was bothersome to other experts, who noted that the pages they could see did not look like typical diary entries. "When you look at the pages," said one, "you find that the writer never changed his mind. It all looks too perfect. That's not how people write."[71]

"Very Limited Understanding"

As suspicious as those impressions were, however, historians were far more bothered by the actual content of the diaries. To those who were experts on the Hitler era of Germany, it was obvious that the documents had been forged by someone who was not familiar with the details of Hitler's life and who borrowed extensively from one particular book. Entitled *Hitler's Speeches and Proclamations*, it was written by Max Domarus in 1962. Domarus had made several significant errors in his book, and significantly, those same errors appeared in the diaries.

Gerd Heidemann leaves court after being convicted of selling the fake Hitler diaries to Stern.

For example, in the book Domarus described an occasion when German general Franz von Epp congratulated Hitler on his fiftieth birthday in 1937. However, Hitler was only forty-eight years old at the time. What Domarus meant to say, in fact, was that Hitler had commended the general on his fiftieth anniversary of army service.

One expert noted that such errors not only all but proved that the diaries were forged, but also revealed what book the forger had referenced to fill out

"I'm Quite Exasperating for the Police"

Author Charles Hamilton explains what happened to Konrad Kujau, the forger of the Hitler diaries, after the forgery was uncovered.

The amiable little con man who threw the world into a turmoil, Konrad "Conny" Kujau, was detained longer than expected in prison. He is now free and is doing what he loves most to do—forging—but this time on the right side of the law. He owns a "Gallery of Fakes" in Stuttgart where he offers "renditions" of paintings by his favorite artists: Renoir, Rembrandt, van Gogh, Chagall. . . . On all of Kujau's paintings appear forged signatures of the masters, but Conny makes it clear that these are not exact copies of works by the great artists. They are, he says, merely artistic improvisations of the artists' motifs done with identical brush strokes.

Kujau also takes special orders from his customers. "You tell me the subject and name of the artist," he tells them, "and I'll paint just like him." . . .

"I'm quite exasperating for the police," admits Conny.

Many people have been fooled by the work of Konrad Kujau.

Charles Hamilton, *The Hitler Diaries: Fakes That Fooled the World*, Lexington: University Press of Kentucky, 1991, p. 189.

the entries in the sixty-two notebooks. He pointed out that the dates for which Domarus had written nothing were also blank in the diaries . "You get the impression," he said, "of a very limited understanding from a person who had an interest in making entries only when Domarus did."[72]

Forensic Science Agrees

Soon after the historians weighed in with their opinions, the Federal Archives scientists delivered their verdict—forgery. The paper was viewed under ultraviolet light and showed whiteners that did not exist when Hitler was alive. A microscopic analysis showed that the bindings of the notebooks contained threads of a synthetic material called polyester, which was manufactured for the first time in 1953—long after Hitler's death.

The evidence was irrefutable. Once it was shown that the diaries were forged, it was easy to trace them back to the man who had forged them. He was Konrad Kujau, the German memorabilia dealer who had provided them to *Stern*. Kujau had been forging Nazi souvenirs for years, finding that people would pay a small fortune for something with Adolf Hitler's signature on it—and he had provided hundreds of fake documents. Kujau was tried and sentenced to prison for his crimes.

Not surprisingly, the publications that had rushed to print the diaries were embarrassed, especially because it was clear that had they waited until the forensic tests were completed, they could have avoided being so publicly humiliated. Said one *Stern* executive, "We have reason to be ashamed."[73] The scoop of the century had become a nightmare, as the greed of the collector—or in this case, the publisher—had become the forger's most valuable ally.

CHAPTER 5

"Ancient" Fakes

A final type of forgery is that of what are known as antiquities—relics or objects from ancient times. As with art forgery investigations, those who investigate the authenticity of antiquities are usually not police. Instead, scientists, historians, and archaeologists are consulted, and while they often use some of the same investigative tools, they also may bring to the investigation specific knowledge and equipment that law enforcement may not have.

A Giant on Stub Newell's Farm

One of the most famous forgeries of antiquities in the United States took place in 1869, long before today's sensitive instruments were available to forensic technicians. Known as the Cardiff giant, it was discovered in 1869 by two men digging a well on William "Stub" Newell's farm in Cardiff, New York. The giant was a 10-foot-long (3m) stone figure of a man, and understandably caused a great stir in the little town.

People assumed it was a petrified man from prehistoric days, and flocked to Newell's farm to see it. Realizing he could make some money from the relic, Newell erected a tent over the giant and charged people a quarter to see it. He doubled the price after two days, and people kept arriving.

Andrew White, the president of Cornell University, described his visit to see the giant. "The roads were crowded with buggies, carriages, and even omnibuses from the city, and with lumber-wagons from the farms—all laden with passengers." The giant, White wrote, was very impressive: "Lying in its grave, with the subdued light from the roof of the tent falling upon it, and with the limbs contorted as if in a death

The Cardiff Giant, a famous hoax of a petrified man, is disinterred from its New York grave in 1869.

struggle, it produced a most weird effect. An air of great solemnity pervaded the place. Visitors hardly spoke above a whisper."[74]

A Hunk of Gypsum

The giant did appear human. Long dark streaks looked like veins, and tiny pores showed in what apparently once was skin. The truth, however, was that it was a forgery, and Stub Newell's cousin, George Hull, was behind it. Hull said that while the money was an added bonus, his motivation was to poke fun at an annoying preacher he had recently met.

The man told Hull that it was important to take literally every story in the Bible, even the strange ones, such as the one in Genesis that talked about giants once roaming on the earth. "I suddenly thought of making a stone giant," he later admitted, "and passing it off as a petrified man."[75]

He wanted to do this secretly, so he traveled to Iowa and found a large 12-foot-long (3.7m) hunk of gypsum. He hired a stonecutter to fashion it into a man, and told him to pound the statue's exterior with steel needles hammered into wooden blocks to give the appearance of pores. Hull also used sulfuric acid to make the statue look discolored, as prehistoric remains might look.

Hull paid more than two thousand dollars for the giant to be shipped to Cardiff, where he and Newell quietly buried it in a shallow grave behind the barn. After a year, Newell hired two men to dig a well, knowing that they would discover the giant.

"Old Hoaxey"

A month after the discovery, a group of businessmen paid Hull twenty-three thousand dollars for the giant and moved it to Syracuse, New York, to be put on permanent display. There, it was examined more thoroughly by experts. One noted Yale

Curious onlookers watch the unearthing of the Cardiff Giant.

"Old Hoaxey," lies in its pen at the Farmer's Museum in Cooperstown, New York.

paleontologist, a specialist in fossils, announced that it could not have been human—and was not even a very good forgery.

He noted the chisel marks from its carving and said that if the statue had been in the ground for thousands of years, the marks would definitely have worn away. "It is of very recent origin," he said, "and a most decided humbug. . . . I am surprised that any scientific observers should not have at once detected the unmistakable evidence against its antiquity."[76]

Soon afterward Hull and Newell confessed, but surprisingly, public interest grew after the forgery was revealed. People referred to the giant affectionately as "Old Hoaxey," and it was eventually given a permanent location in the Farmer's Museum in Cooperstown, New York.

Tool Markings as Clues

The use of tool markings has been used by others to reveal forgeries of antiquities—and in increasingly high-tech ways. Art and antiquities expert Jane MacLaren Walsh, who has investigated a number of ancient artifacts from various archaeological digs in Mexico, has found that one of the best ways to authenticate an ancient artifact is to understand the tools that were available when it was supposedly created. One of the biggest giveaways in a forged artifact, she says, is lines and holes that are too perfect. "With modern tools, you get these regular, clean lines, very sharp and narrow," she says. "If you see impressions left by a tool that didn't exist [at the time], you know it is a fake."[77]

She has experimented with likely materials that were available in ancient times. For example, obsidian—a glass created by the intense heat of a volcano—is extremely hard and would have been a valuable tool. In addition, the sharpened bones of small animals like mice and rabbits might have been used to create holes in artifacts. Walsh knows, because she herself has cleaned and sharpened such materials and has tried using them as drill bits, much as ancient people might have done. Such experimentation has allowed her to make a database of likely tools and the marks they leave in authentic artifacts.

A forged crystal skull purportedly carved by the ancient Aztecs was purchased by the British Museum in 1897.

A Crystal Skull

Her work has become known to archaeological investigators all over the world. One 2005 case, for example, involved a life-size crystal skull believed to have been carved by the ancient Aztecs. It had been held by the British Museum in London since 1897, but some art experts had expressed doubt that it was real. One researcher felt the crystal was polished to an extent beyond what an ancient artist could have done.

"When you look at known, genuine Aztec rock crystals," he explained, "they have a much gentler polish. This has the harsh, polished look you get with modern equipment."[78] The researchers wanted to look more closely at tool marks left on the skull, and they consulted with Walsh.

Faint inscriptions show on this ancient jar. Forgers sometimes add inscriptions to artifacts in hopes of increasing their value.

The Scanning Electron Microscope

The first step was to make a mold of the skull's surface. They used resin, the substance dentists use when making an exact impression of a tooth. After the material was set, they viewed it under a powerful scanning electron microscope, or SEM. The SEM works by firing a beam of electrons over the sur-

face of the object—in this case, the mold of the skull's surface. As the electrons in the beam hit the mold, they kick up other electrons on its surface, and they scatter.

The image or pattern created by this scattering is relayed to a computer, which displays the image on its screen. The SEM can show in the most minute detail any scratches, cracks, or other marks on the surface in a clear, three-dimensional picture.

What the researchers saw in the SEM scan were the most minuscule scratch marks in the skull's teeth and eye sockets. The scratches had the pattern of a rotary tool—a wheel used by jewelers in the nineteenth century. Noted Walsh, "No pre-Columbian carver ever had such a tool."[79]

That evidence more than established that the skull was a forgery. However, because it was done in the nineteenth century, there was no question of prosecuting the forger. Many experts say that simply establishing whether a piece is forged or real is enough. "Knowing something has been forged breaks the chain," says Moree, a graduate student in archaeology.

A fraud was perpetrated—in this case on the academic community. A forger made it and sold it. . . . And people, for a time, believed it was real and studied it, trying to put it in some historical context.

That was wasted time and energy. But when the fraud is exposed—in this case, a forgery that happened long ago—it breaks that chain. An artifact shown to be forged can't be sold again, and won't be studied or looked at in a historical context. It happens, and it's too bad, but I'm sure it won't be the last.[80]

Measuring the Glow

There are other methods investigators use when trying to learn whether an artifact is genuine. If it is ceramic, scientists can use a technique called thermoluminescence to establish whether the artifact is as old as it is claimed to be.

Thermoluminescence is based on the fact that everything on Earth has a small amount of radiation, simply because cosmic rays are continually pelting Earth's atmosphere. When something made of clay is fired—the process that turns clay hard—it loses that radiation. Afterward, however, it gradually begins to absorb radiation again.

By measuring the amount of radiation in ceramics, a scientist is able to determine the age of the artifact. To perform thermoluminescence, a technician takes a small sample of the ceramic artifact and heats it at a very high temperature, above 640° F (338° C). The intense heat makes the ceramic glow, and by measuring the level of glowing, scientists can tell how much radiation is in the piece—and therefore, how many years have passed since it was originally fired.

Disproving Dossena's *Diana*

Thermoluminescence has been used in investigating several ancient Greek and Roman statues and pottery shards. One of the most famous turned out to be also one of the best forgeries of an antiquity ever created—a statue of Diana, the Roman goddess of the hunt.

It had supposedly been found in an archeological dig site in Italy, and experts were amazed at its detail and artistry—even though it was in twenty-one separate pieces. It was believed to have been sculpted in the sixth century B.C. In 1952 the St. Louis Art Museum in Missouri purchased the statue from a Los Angeles art dealer for fifty-six thousand dollars. The museum directors were thrilled at the new addition to their collection, saying that the statue "is one of the most important revelations of the art of antiquity made in the twentieth century."[81]

Soon, however, the publicity caught the eye of Harold Woodbury Parsons, a Boston art investigator, who suspected the statue was a forgery by a man named Alceo Dossena. Museums and collectors around the world continued to be fooled by Dossena forgeries, even though Dossena had been dead since 1937. In addition to forging ceramic pieces, Dossena created other types of fake antiquities including stone sculptures. He was particularly cunning in his use of what he believed was a secret formula to age the stone pieces he created. He dipped them repeatedly in a mixture of chemicals that would replicate the normal deterioration of the surface of material buried and exposed to the elements.

Museum officials, dreading the idea that their newest acquisition would turn out to be a forgery, reluctantly agreed to do a thermoluminescence test. A tiny amount of the clay was removed from the base with a dental drill and heated rapidly. The light given off by the sample was then measured, and technicians were able to render the verdict. Rather than more than twenty-five hundred years old, the statue was shown to be only about forty, and thus, a forgery.

Dossena Outs Himself

Alceo Dossena was such a talented forger that no one was able to catch him at it—at least until he turned himself in. Dossena had gone into business with an antiques dealer named Romano Palesi, who was good at inventing interesting provenances for Dossena's fakes. Palesi told Dossena that he could easily sell as many fake antiquities as Dossena could turn out.

What he had not told Dossena, however, was that he was taking 80 percent of the money paid for Dossena's hard work. In 1927 Dossena was shocked to learn that Palesi had sold one of his forgeries for $150,000, and had given Dossena only $7,500. Enraged, Dossena went to court and tried to sue his partner. Although the suit was never settled, Dossena was willing to admit to the forgeries rather than have someone cheat him.

The Piltdown Forgery

A most famous forgery that was finally solved because of a dating technique was that of the Piltdown Man. This was a skull

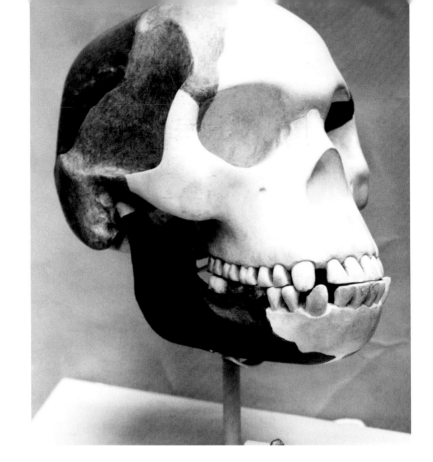

The skull known as Piltdown Man appeared to be the missing link between apes and humans until it was revealed to be a forgery.

found in 1912 by an amateur paleontologist, or fossil collector, named Charles Dawson. Dawson was digging in a gravel pit near Piltdown, an area in the south of England, when he and a friend unearthed what appeared to be large fragments of an ancient skull and, nearby, its jawbone. Dawson and his companion also uncovered crude tools made of animal bone. The tools, skull, and jawbone were dirty and stained, indicating they had lain in the earth a long time.

What made this such an extraordinary find was that while the skull looked human, the jawbone was more like that of an ape. Since 1859, when Charles Darwin had put forth his theory of evolution in which he proposed that humans had developed from apes, scientists had been searching for some proof. Could this skull with its characteristics of both human and ape be the missing link?

Dawson's friend Arthur Smith Woodward, head of the Department of Geology at the British Museum, was able to show how the jaw and skull fit together. Writes one researcher, "It had a thick, remarkably big brain case—almost the size of modern man's—looming incongruously over the large, primitive jaw of an ape."[82] Most interesting was that though the jaw was clearly apelike, its molars were worn. This was significant, because apes do not grind with their back teeth as humans do. Woodward concluded that the skull belonged to a human-like creature that used rudimentary tools. This creature did seem to be that missing link between human and ape.

Skepticism

Not everyone in the scientific community agreed with this theory, however. Some felt that the skull and jawbone were so dissimilar that they could not possibly belong together. Others wondered why, with so much archaeological digging that had occurred, no other such skulls with apelike jawbones had been recovered.

There were no scientific tests available in the early 1900s, so the Piltdown discoveries continued to be regarded as possible proof of Darwin's theory of evolution. However, beginning in 1949, the Piltdown Man was viewed again by scientists, who this time were armed with new types of investigative methods.

One method measured the amount of an element called fluorine in the skull and jawbone. Fluorine is found in groundwater throughout the world. Material such as the skull and jawbone at Piltdown that has been lying in pits gradually soaks in fluorine from the damp soil, and over time this changes the chemical composition of the bones. When the level of fluorine in a sample of bone is measured, scientists can offer an accurate estimate of how long that bone has been underground.

In the case of the Piltdown finds, the fluorine levels of the skull and jawbone were very different. While the test showed that the skull was about fifty thousand years old, the jawbone was much newer. Further study showed that it belonged, as some skeptics had suspected, to a modern orangutan, and had been stained to match the skull. The teeth, they also discovered, had been filed down to give the appearance of human molars. Finally, a microscopic look at the tools found with the bones showed that they had been shaped and sharpened with metal instruments—more proof that they had been planted relatively recently.

"No Parallel"

The testing that began in 1949 showed beyond a doubt that the scientific community had been duped. Those who did the testing admitted that they had been the victim of an elaborate hoax. Time, energy, and money had been spent in studying the Piltdown remains, and for more than forty years the discovery had shaped the scientific thinking of the time.

As for who the forger was, no one knows for certain. Many believe it was Charles Dawson, since he found the remains. Money was not the motive, since the skull and other artifacts were not sold. Perhaps, experts theorize, it was a desire to have his name attached to an exciting archaeological find. As the *London Times* wrote in 1953, "It would be but one more instance of desire for fame . . . leading a scholar into dishonesty."[83]

Less Destructive Tests

While determining an artifact's age is often the most important way of proving it a forgery, it has usually been necessary to damage the artifact somewhat in testing it. This is risky because brittle fossils, pottery, bones, and other antiquities can break as investigators drill a sample from the base of a statue or scrape the surface of an ancient bone in order to authenticate it.

However, in recent years more and more medical instruments have been applied to forensic investigations of antiquities. Many of the machines used to diagnose illnesses are what scientists call "noninvasive," which means that they can measure or scan without doing injury or harm to the patient.

Some of the most interesting work is being done with CAT scanners, which have usually been used in hospitals to help

doctors get a three-dimensional look inside a patient. Unlike a traditional X-ray machine, the CAT scanner shows soft tissue—and as a result, doctors can view details of a faulty heart valve, for example, or get a clear view of a tumor.

In the same way, the CAT scanner digitally images artifacts and can present a three-dimensional view on a screen. This scanner used to check for forgeries is far more powerful than its medical counterpart. "The problem with [our using] medical CAT scanners," notes one expert, "is that they're specifically engineered not to kill anybody. That's something you

In this 1953 picture, a scientist explains the features that confirm the recent origin of the Piltdown skull.

A fifteenth-century sculpture enters a CAT scanner. CAT scanners have helped researchers authenticate fossils and thwart forgers.

don't have to worry about when you're doing inanimate objects like fossils and things like that. As a result, we can use higher energy x-rays and image for a much longer time."[84]

A Forged Fossil

A recent case demonstrates how valuable a CAT scanner can be in detecting a forgery of a fossil. While those who are not familiar with the world of paleontology may not realize it, collectors sometimes spend millions of dollars on a single specimen. Not surprisingly then, it is not difficult to understand why forgers might attempt to create fakes.

Paleontologist Timothy Rowe tells of a researcher who brought into the lab a fossil that was quite unusual. It seemed to be a complete skull of a tiny monkey—a perfect specimen, he says, "uncrushed, still in the rock matrix, jaws slightly open and all this cranium that held its brain is complete."[85] The researcher wanted Rowe to test the fossil—not to see if it was authentic, because he was certain that it was—but to see in close-up detail what the interior of the tiny monkey's skull looked like.

After just a few scans with the CAT scanner, however, Rowe could see that the fossil was a forgery. Though the rock in which the fossil was embedded was real, says Rowe, "we could see that [the fossil itself] was sculpted out of a dental amalgam and the whole thing was a setup to look like a little skull still embedded in the matrix."[86] Since the motive for the forgery was profit, the researcher could at least begin to get his money back by tracing the fossil to the dealer who sold it.

The Forgery Museum in Germany (pictured) has a most unusual collection. It houses and collects forgeries of all kinds.

Staying Close

But no matter how good investigators are or how sensitive and accurate their machines, it is unlikely that forgery can ever be stopped. Greed—whether for money or fame—is a powerful motivator, and it has been driving forgers for centuries.

Even so, there is no doubt that the application of new technology can speed up forgery investigations. And forgery experts say that whether the fake is a counterfeit check or a phony Rembrandt, the quicker it can be exposed as a forgery, the more likely it is that investigators can trace it to its source. "It's a question of staying within a few steps of a forger or [check] counterfeiter," says one police officer. "If investigators can stay that close, they have a great chance of catching these folks before they victimize someone else.[87]

Notes

Introduction: An Almost Invisible Crime

1. Patricia, interview with the author, Eden Prairie, Minnesota, February 19, 2006.

2. Quoted in Greg Risling, "Home Run Ends Up a Foul Ball," *Wisconsin State Journal*, February 24, 2006, p. B1.

3. Quoted in Oriana Zill, "Crossing Borders: How Terrorists Use Fake Passports, Visas, and Other Identity Documents," *PBS Frontline*. www.pbs.org/wgbh/pages/frontline/shows/trail/etc/fake.html.

4. Tony, interview with the author, Minneapolis, Minnesota, March 1, 2006.

5. Steve Kincaid, interview with the author, Minneapolis, MN March 10, 2006.

6. Dave, interview with the author, Minneapolis, Minnesota, March 4, 2005.

Chapter 1: Forging and Bank Fraud

7. Gary, interview with the author, Deephaven, Minnesota, February 27, 2006.

8. Gary, interview with the author.

9. Vicki Colliander, interview with the author, Lake Elmo, Minnesota, March 3, 2006.

10. Terry, interview with the author, Minneapolis, Minnesota, March 3, 2006.

11. Kincaid, interview with the author.

12. Colliander, interview with the author.

13. Joleen, telephone interview with the author, February 28, 2006.

14. Colliander, interview with the author.

15. Quoted in Sam Skolnik, "Meth Use Linked to Jump in ID, Mail Thefts," *Seattle Post-Intelligencer*, July 23, 2001, p. 1A.

16. Jesse, interview with the author, Minneapolis, Minnesota, February 28, 2006.

17. Terry, interview with the author, Minneapolis, Minnesota, March 16, 2006.

18. Colliander, interview with the author.

19. Tony, interview with the author.

20. Quoted in David Chanen, "Police Working to Stop Check Ring," *Minneapolis Star Tribune*, April 29, 2000, p. 1A.

21. Colliander, interview with the author.

22. Edith, interview with the author, Minneapolis, Minnesota, March 30, 2006.

23. Cray, telephone interview with the author, March 2, 2006.

24. Colliander, interview with the author.

25. Kincaid, interview with the author.

26. Kincaid, interview with the author.

27. Dave C., interview with the author, St. Paul, Minnesota, November 4, 2005.

28. Colliander, interview with the author.

Chapter 2: Art Forgery

29. Quoted in Walter McCrone, "Artful Dodgers," *Sciences*, January/February 2001, p. 32.

30. Quoted in McCrone, "Artful Dodgers," p. 32.

31. Terry Zech, interview with the author, Bloomington, Minnesota, March 31, 2006.

32. Quoted in Jonathan Jones, "Forgery's Great Renaissance," *Manchester Guardian*, April 25, 1998, p. 4.

33. Thomas Hoving, *False Impressions: The Hunt For Big-Time Art Fakes*. New York: Simon & Schuster, 1996, p. 330.

34. Hoving, *False Impressions*, p. 16.

35. Janice, telephone interview with the author, Minneapolis, Minnesota, April 1, 2005.

36. Quoted in McCrone, "Artful Dodgers," p. 32.

37. Quoted in Giles Tremlett, "Briton Exposes Fakes Among Prado Goyas," *Manchester Guardian*, April 5, 2001, p. 1.15.

38. Quoted in *Benchmark*, "Art Forgeries," no. 3, 2004.

39. Doris Athineos, "Phony Provenances Shake the Art World," *Forbes*, August 12, 1996, p. 168.

40. Quoted in Brian Innes, *Fakes & Forgeries: The True Crime Stories of History's Greatest Deceptions*. Pleasantville, NY: Reader's Digest, 2005, p. 87.

41 McCrone, "Artful Dodgers," p. 32.

Chapter 3: Paper, Ink, and Penmanship

42. Julian Arkin, telephone interview with the author, April 6, 2006.

43. Kincaid, interview with the author.

44. Quoted in David Fisher, *Hard Evidence: How Detectives Inside the FBI's Sci-Crime Lab Have Helped Solve America's Toughest Cases*. New York: Simon & Schuster, 1995, p. 200.

45. Charles Hamilton, *Great Forgers and Famous Fakes: The Manuscript Forgers of America & How They Duped the Experts*. New York: Crown, 1980, p. 99.

46. Fisher, *Hard Evidence*, p. 194.

47. Hamilton, *Great Forgers*, p. 265.

48. Quoted in Joe Nickell, *Detecting Forgery: Forensic Investigation of Documents*. Lexington: University Press of Kentucky, 1996, p. 117.

49. Kenneth Rendell, *Forging History: The Detection of Fake Letters and Documents*. Norman: University of Oklahoma Press, 1994, p. 23.

50. Amy, interview with the author, St. Paul, Minnesota, March 13, 2006.

51. Rendell, *Forging History*, p. 20.

52. Quoted in Rendell, *Forging History*, p. 71.

53. Hamilton, *Great Forgers*, p. 21.

54. Quoted in Hamilton, *Great Forgers*, p. 21.

55. Quoted in Hamilton, *Great Forgers*, p. 21.

56. Arkin, telephone interview with the author.

Chapter 4: Two Expensive Forgeries

57. Hamilton, *Great Forgers*, p. 166.

58. Charlie Johnson, interview with the author, Minneapolis, Minnesota, April 13, 2006.

59. Quoted in Hamilton, *Great Forgers*, p. 168.

60. Quoted in Innes, *Fakes & Forgeries*, p. 124.

61. Quoted in Hamilton, *Great Forgers*, p. 170.

62. Quoted in *New York Times*, "Scientist Is Convinced the Voice Is Authentic," January 10, 1972, p. 23.

63. Quoted in Douglas Robinson, "Author Says Voice Was Not Hughes's," *New York Times*, January 11, 1972, p. 1.

64. Quoted in "Scientist Is Convinced Voice Is Authentic," p. 23.

65. Quoted in *Time*, "Hitler's Forged Diaries," May 16, 1983, p. 36.

66. Katherine Spanish, telephone interview with the author, April 18, 2006.

67. Quoted in "Hitler's Forged Diaries," p. 36.

68. Quoted in *Newsweek*, "Cracking the Case," May 16, 1983, p. 58.

69. Quoted in *Newsweek*, "Cracking the Case," p. 59.

70. Quoted in *Newsweek*, "Cracking the Case," p. 60.

71. Quoted in *Newsweek*, "Cracking the Case," p. 57.

72. Charles Hamilton, *The Hitler Diaries: Fakes That Fooled the World*, Lexington: University Press of Kentucky, 1991, p. 98.

73. Quoted in *Newsweek*, "Cracking the Case," p. 56.

Chapter 5: "Ancient" Fakes

74. Quoted in Mark Rose, "When Giants Roamed the Earth," *Archaeology*, November/December 2005, p. 30.

75. Quoted in Rose, "When Giants Roamed the Earth," p. 32.

76. Quoted in Rose, "When Giants Roamed the Earth," p. 32.

77. Quoted in Jacqueline Trescott, "Separating the Pretend from the Pre-Columbian," *Los Angeles Times*, April 22, 2005, p. E26.

78. Quoted in Mark Vallen, "The Mystery of the Aztec Crystal Skull," *Xispas*, February 2005. xispas.com/art/aztec skull/aztecskull/htm.

79. Quoted in Trescott, "Separating the Pretend from the Pre-Columbian," p. E26.

80. Moree, interview with the author, St. Paul, Minnesota, April 14, 2006.

81. Quoted in editors of Time-Life *Hoaxes and Deceptions*, Alexandria, VA: Time-Life, 1991, p. 25.

82. Quoted in Time-Life, *Hoaxes and Deceptions*, p. 122.

83. *London Times*, "More Doubts on Piltdown Man," November 23, 1953.

84. Quoted in John Nielsen, "Peering Inside Fossils," NPR online, March 10, 2003. www.npr.org/templates/story/story.php?storyid=1183920.

85. Quoted in Joyce Gramza, "On Fakes and Fakers," *ScienCentral News* online, April 8, 2006. www.sciencentral.com/articles/view.php3?article_id=218391539&cat=1_6.

86. Quoted in Gramza, "On Fakes and Fakers."

87. Tony, interview with the author.

For More Information

Books

Frank W. Abagnale, *Catch Me If You Can: The Amazing True Story of the Youngest and Most Daring Con Man in the History of Fun and Profit*. New York: Broadway, 2000. The book upon which the popular movie was based, describing how a teen learned the art of identity theft.

Brian Innes, *Fakes & Forgeries: The True Crime Stories of History's Greatest Deceptions*. Pleasantville, NY: Reader's Digest, 2005. Excellent sections on antiquities and religious forgeries, as well as many color photographs.

Stephanie Nolen, *Shakespeare's Face: Unraveling the Legend and History of Shakespeare's Mysterious Portrait*. New York: Free Press, 2002. A very interesting section on the process of forensic dendrochronology.

Richard Platt, *Crime Scene: The Ultimate Guide to Forensic Science*. New York: DK, 2003. Excellent photographs, with interesting material on the Hitler Diaries investigation.

Internet Sources

Joyce Gramza, "On Fakes and Fakers," *ScienCentral News.com*. April 8, 2006. sciencentral.com/articles/view.php3?arti cle_id=218391539&cat=1_6.

Mark Vallen, "The Mystery of the Aztec Crystal Skull," Xispas.com, February 2005. xispas.com/art/aztecskull/aztecskull.htm.

Oriana Zill, "Crossing Borders: How Terrorists Use Fake Passports, Visas, and Other Identity Documents," *PBS Frontline*. www.pbs.org/wgbh/pages/front line/shows/trail/etc/fake.html.

Video

Steve Drake, *Forensics: Forensic Detectives*, video. Silver Springs, MD: Discovery Channel School, 2001. Excellent information on map forgery and art fraud, with discussion of methods used in testing for forgeries.

Web Sites

A History of Art Forgery (www.mystudios. com/gallery/forgery/history/2.html). Explains why art forgeries are more common than ever, and gives colorful examples of forgeries as well as the scientific methods used in identifying them.

ID Theft (www.consumer.gov/idtheft). This site, run by the Federal Trade Commission, gives current information on the newest scams used by crooks and forgers, as well as helpful information for consumers to guard against identity theft.

Museum of Hoaxes (www.museumof hoaxes.com). From the Hitler diaries to forged antiquities, this site provides hundreds of links to information about some of the most colorful hoaxes and forgeries in history.

Index

Picture Credits

Cover: © CORBIS

About the Author

Gail B. Stewart received her undergraduate degree from Gustavus Adolphus College in St. Peter, Minnesota. She did her graduate work in English, linguistics, and curriculum study at the College of St. Thomas and the University of Minnesota. She taught English and reading for more than ten years.

She has written over ninety books for young people, including a series for Lucent Books called The Other America. She has written many books on historical topics such as World War I and the Warsaw ghetto.

Stewart and her husband live in Minneapolis with their three sons, Ted, Elliot, and Flynn; two dogs; and a cat. When Stewart is not writing, she enjoys reading, walking, and watching her sons play soccer.